I0483171

❧TEEN❧
COLORING BOOKS
MUSIC

Sample Preview

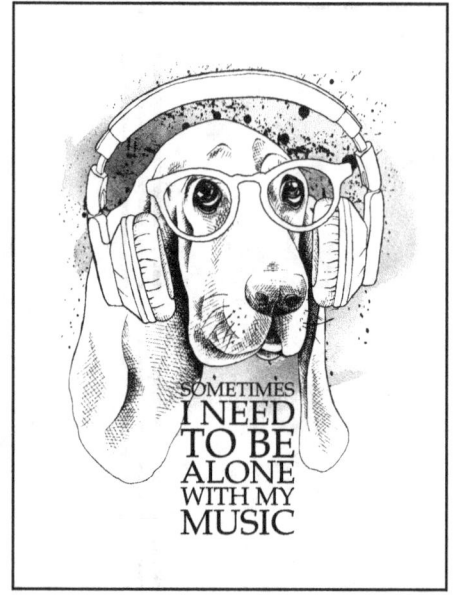

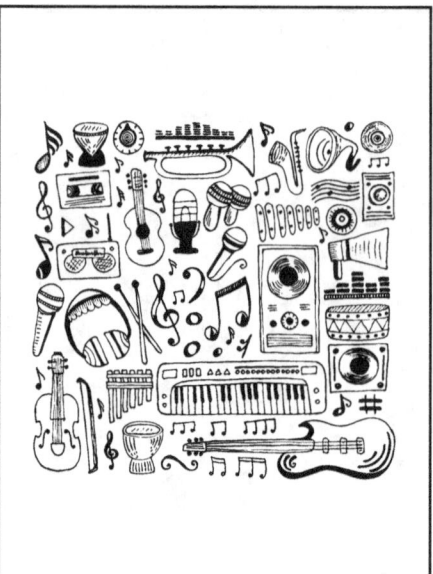

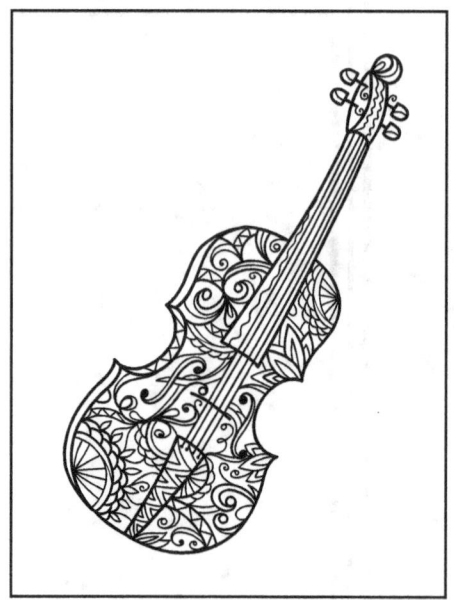

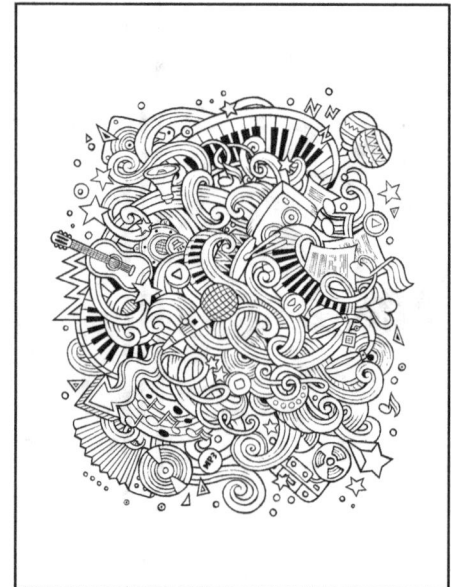

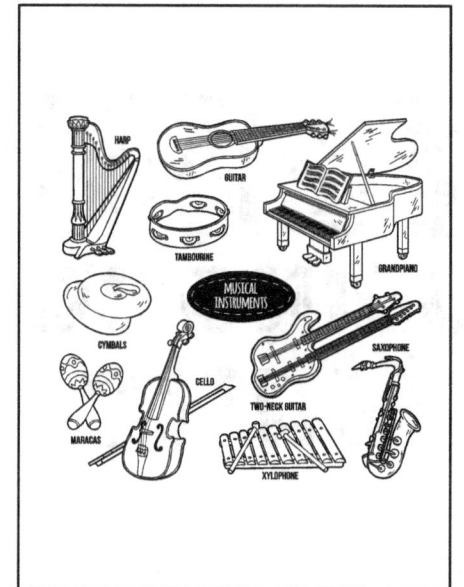

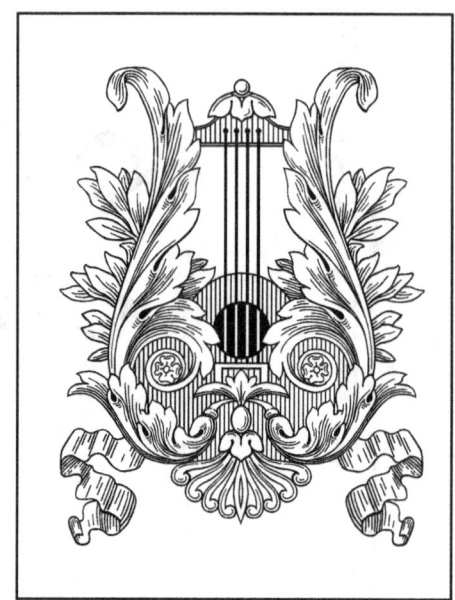

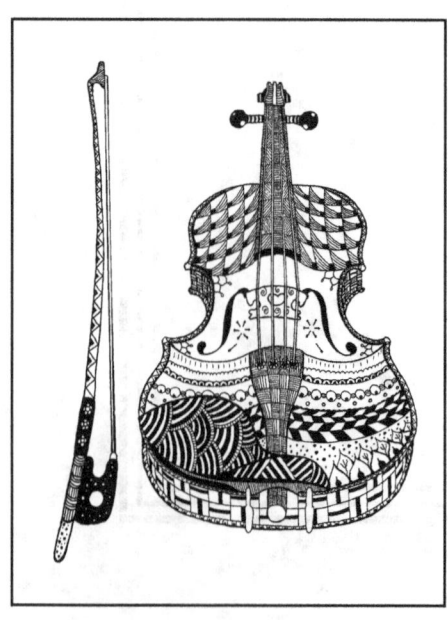

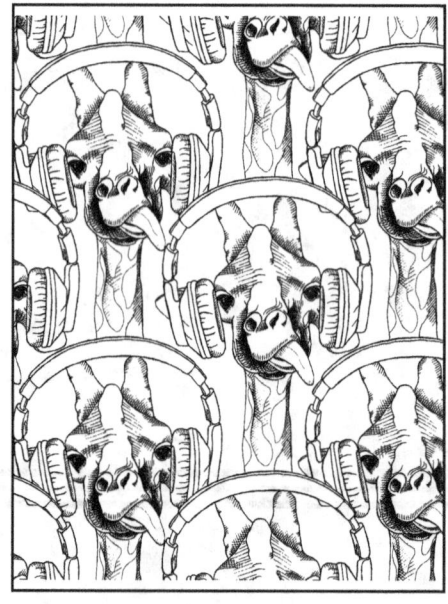

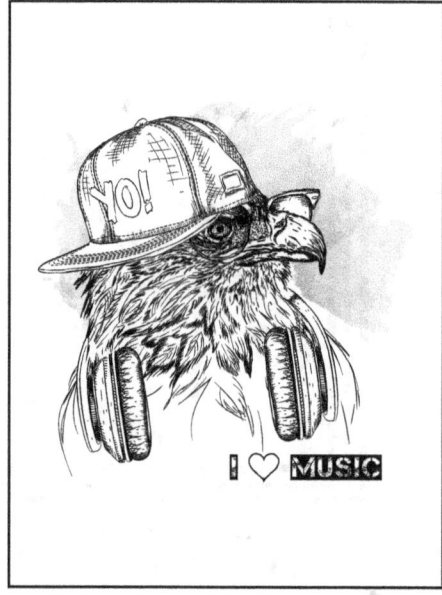

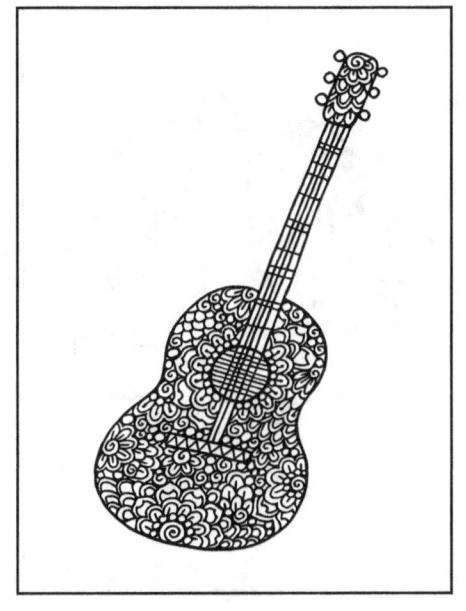
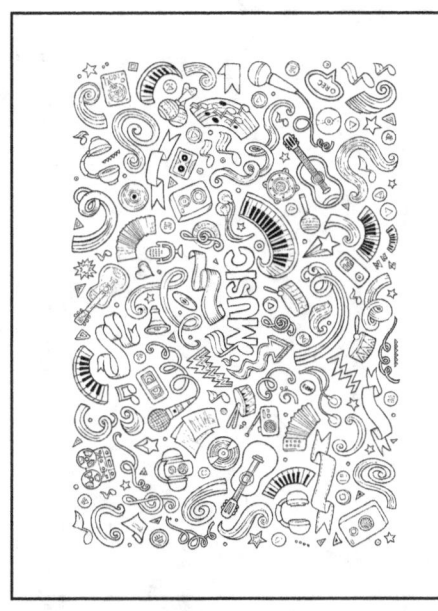
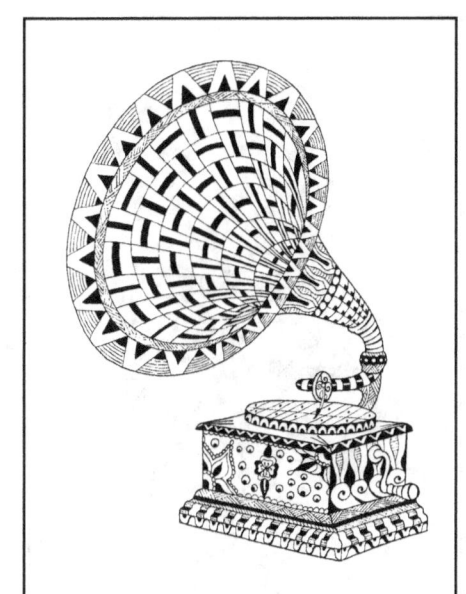
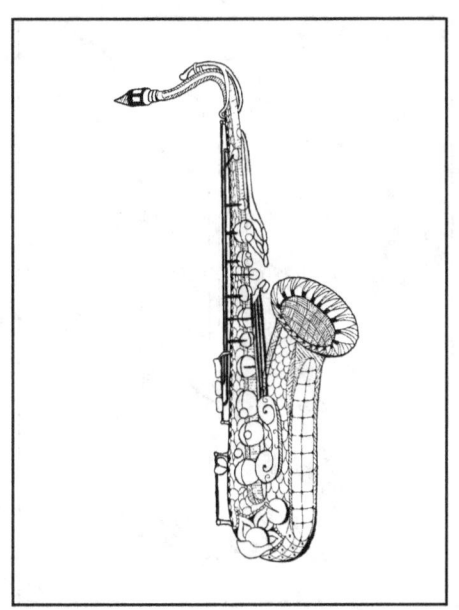
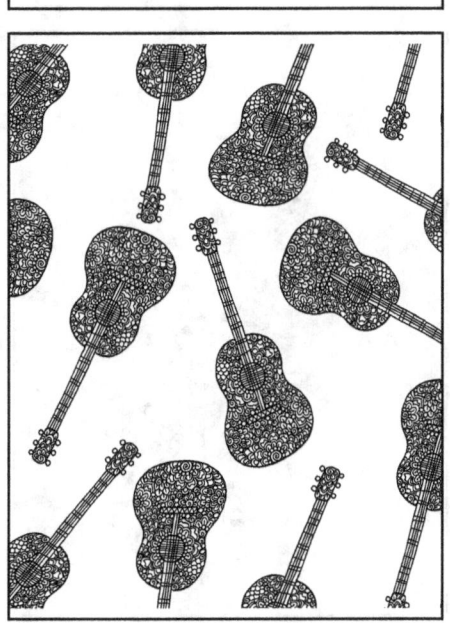
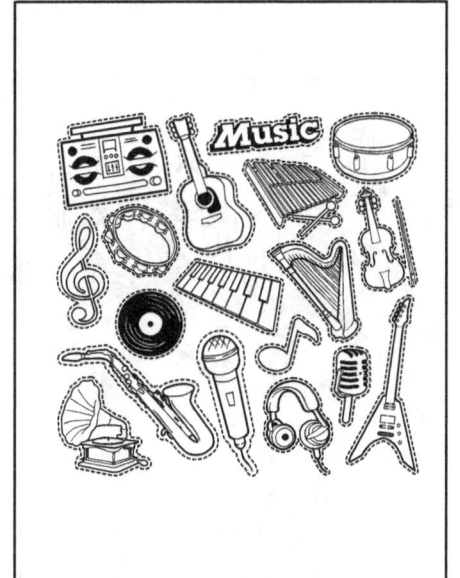
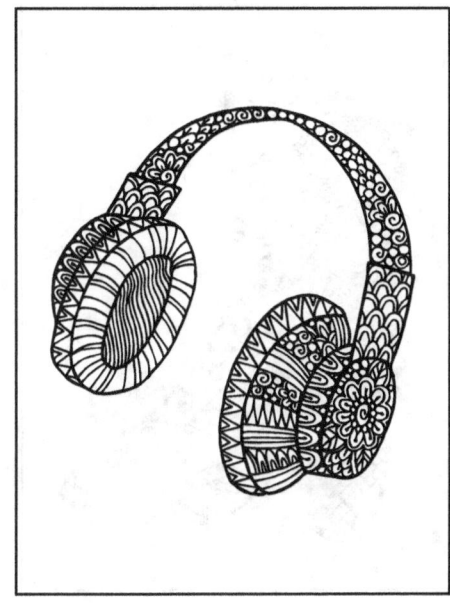
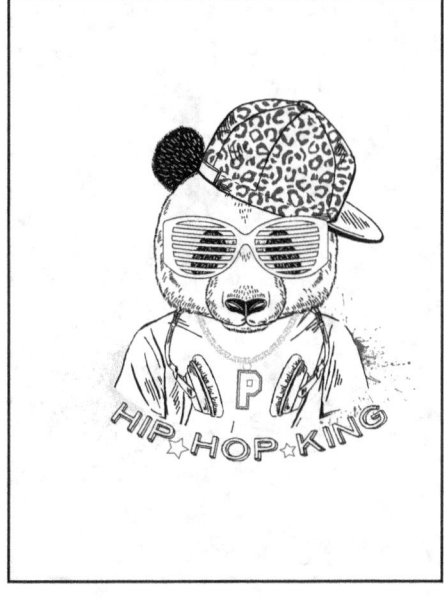
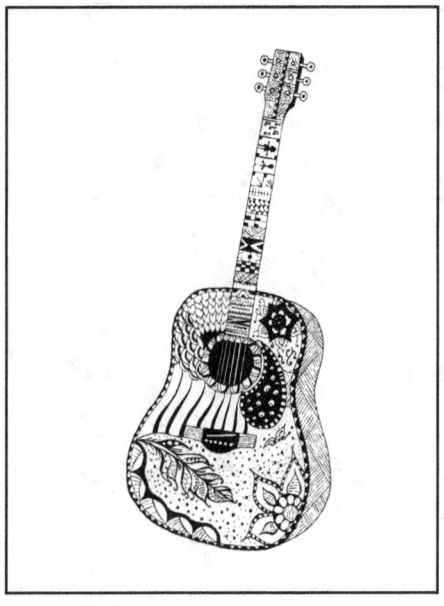

Sample Preview

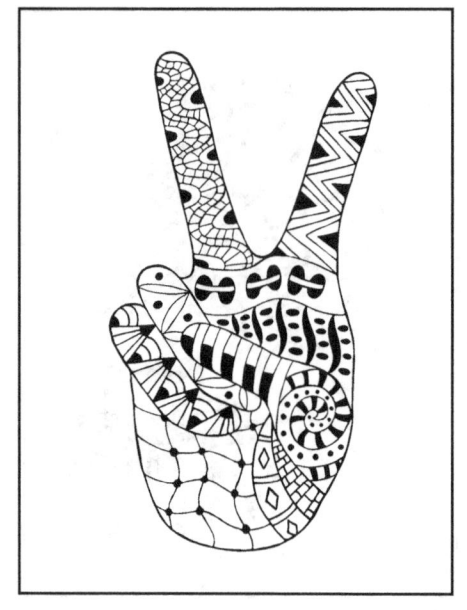
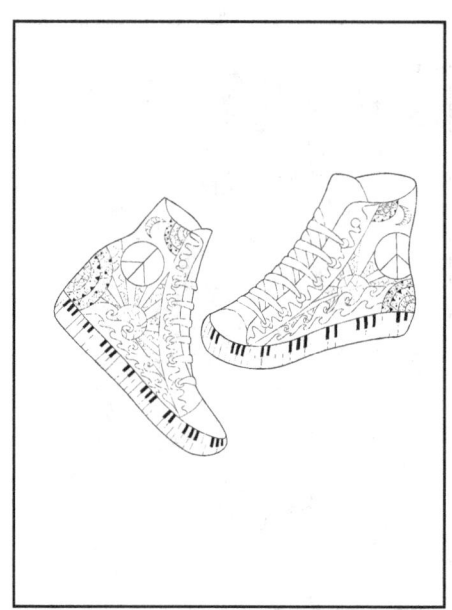
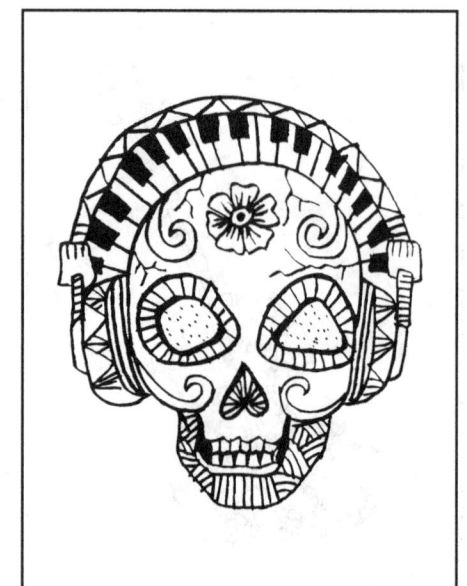
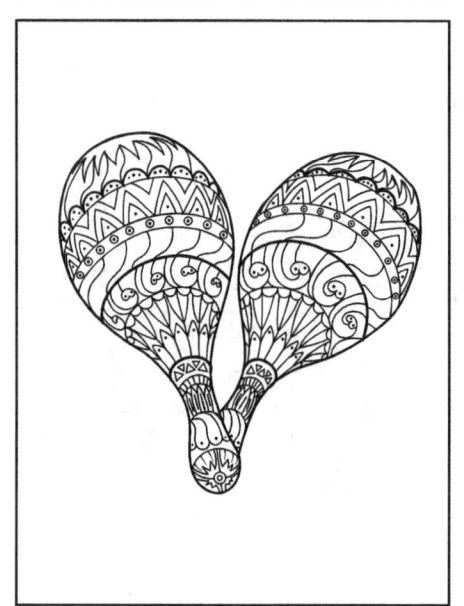
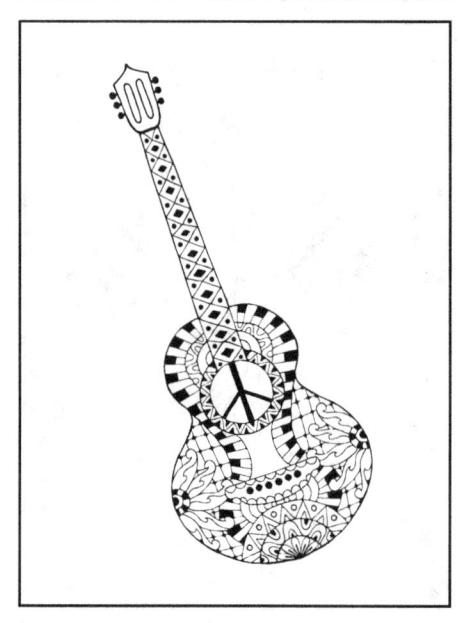
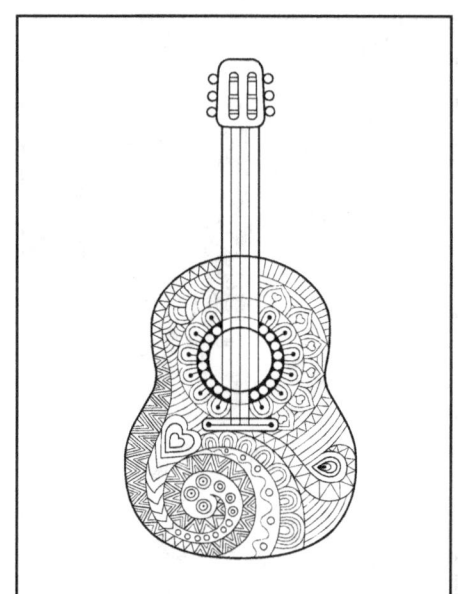
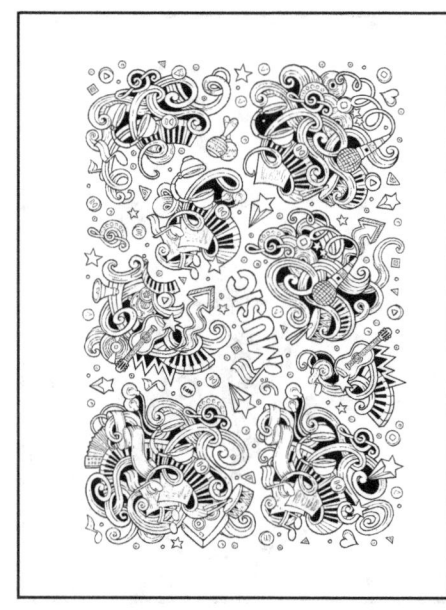
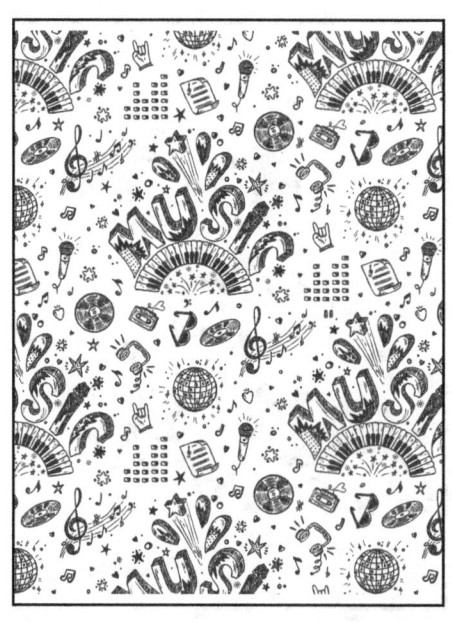
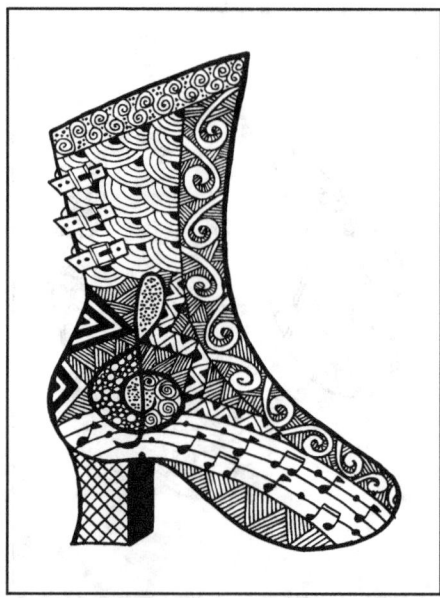

ArtTherapyColoring.com

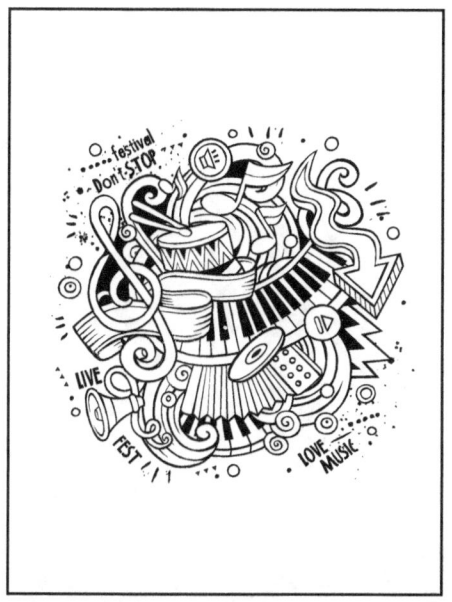

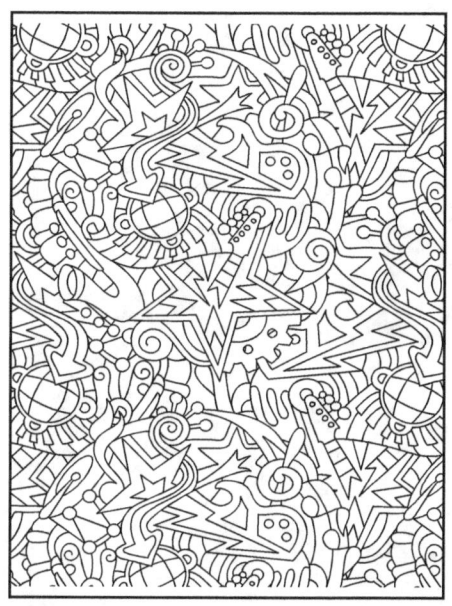

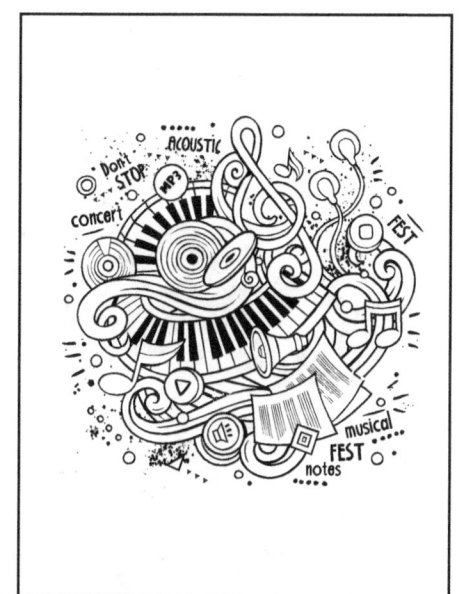

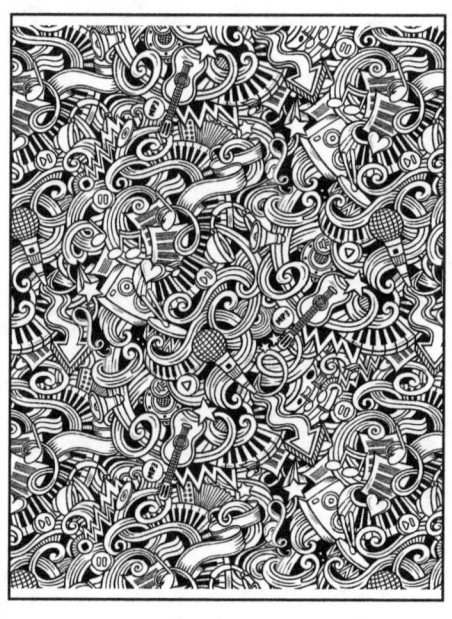

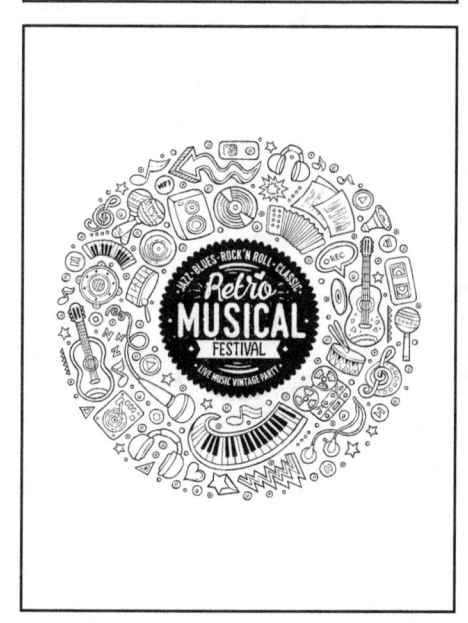

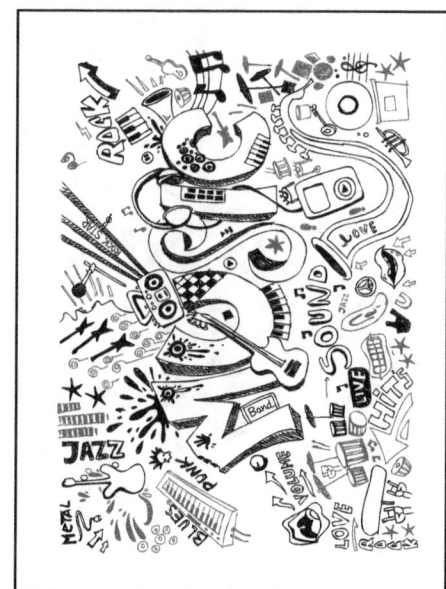

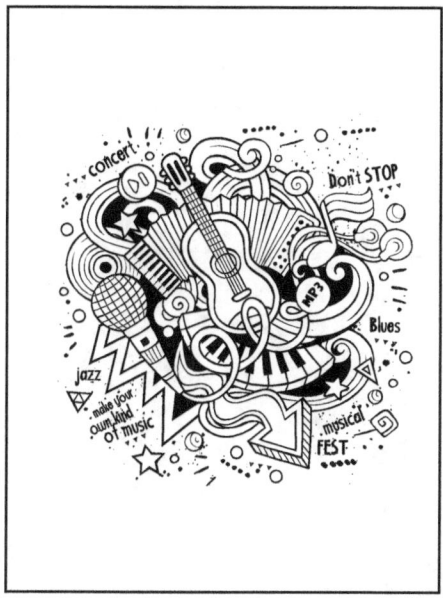

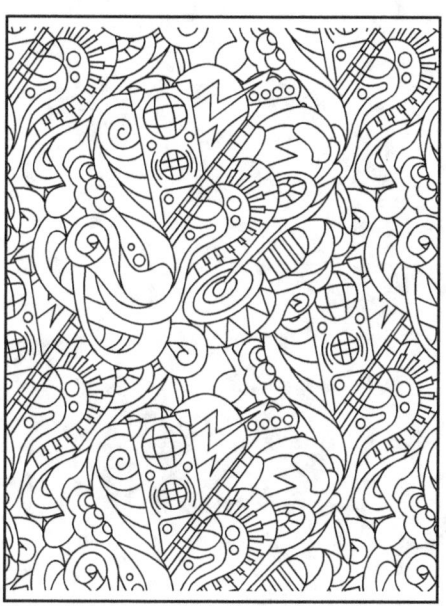

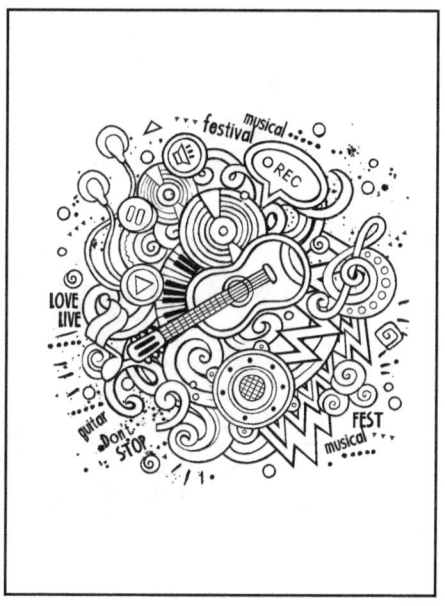

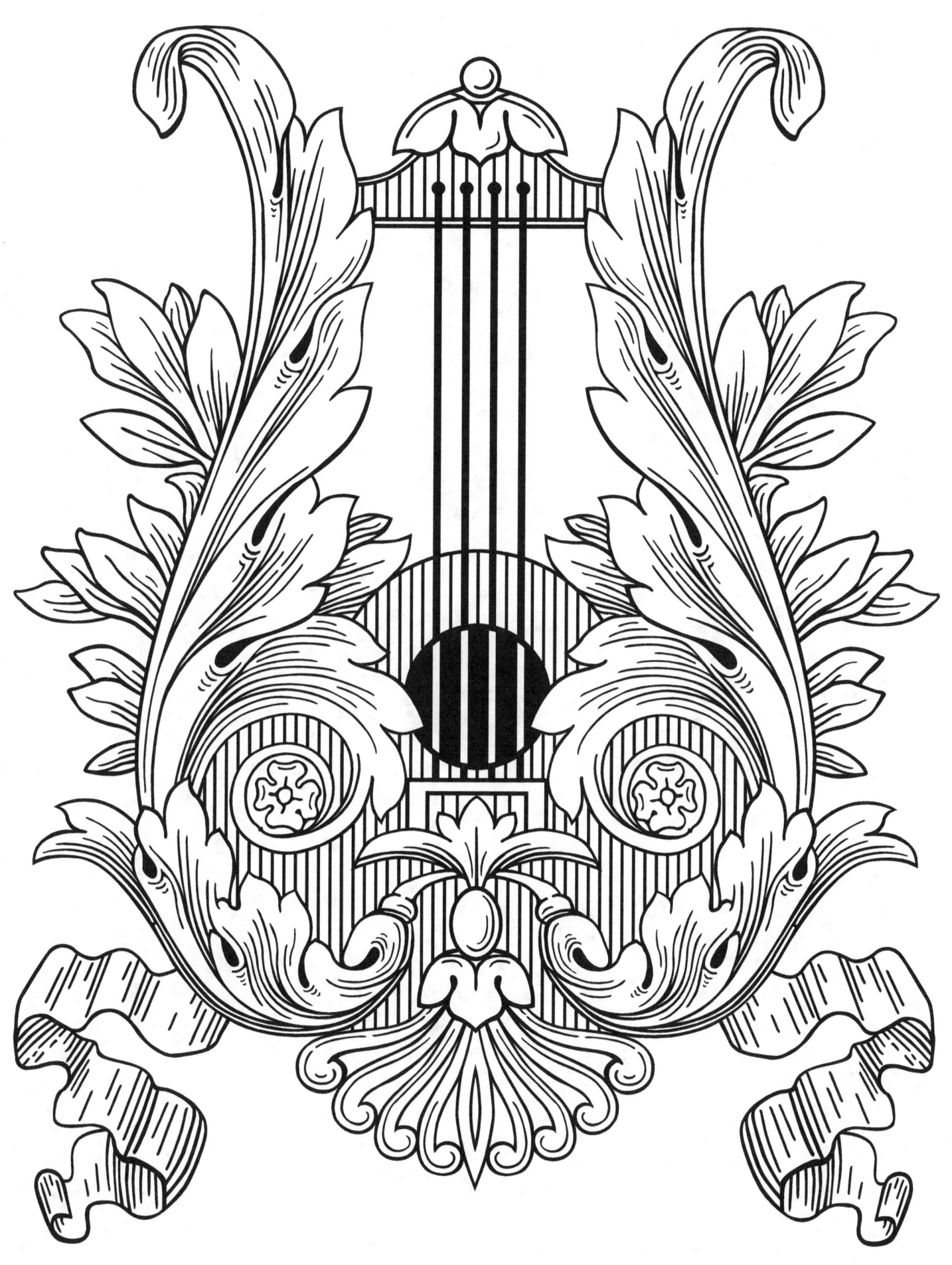

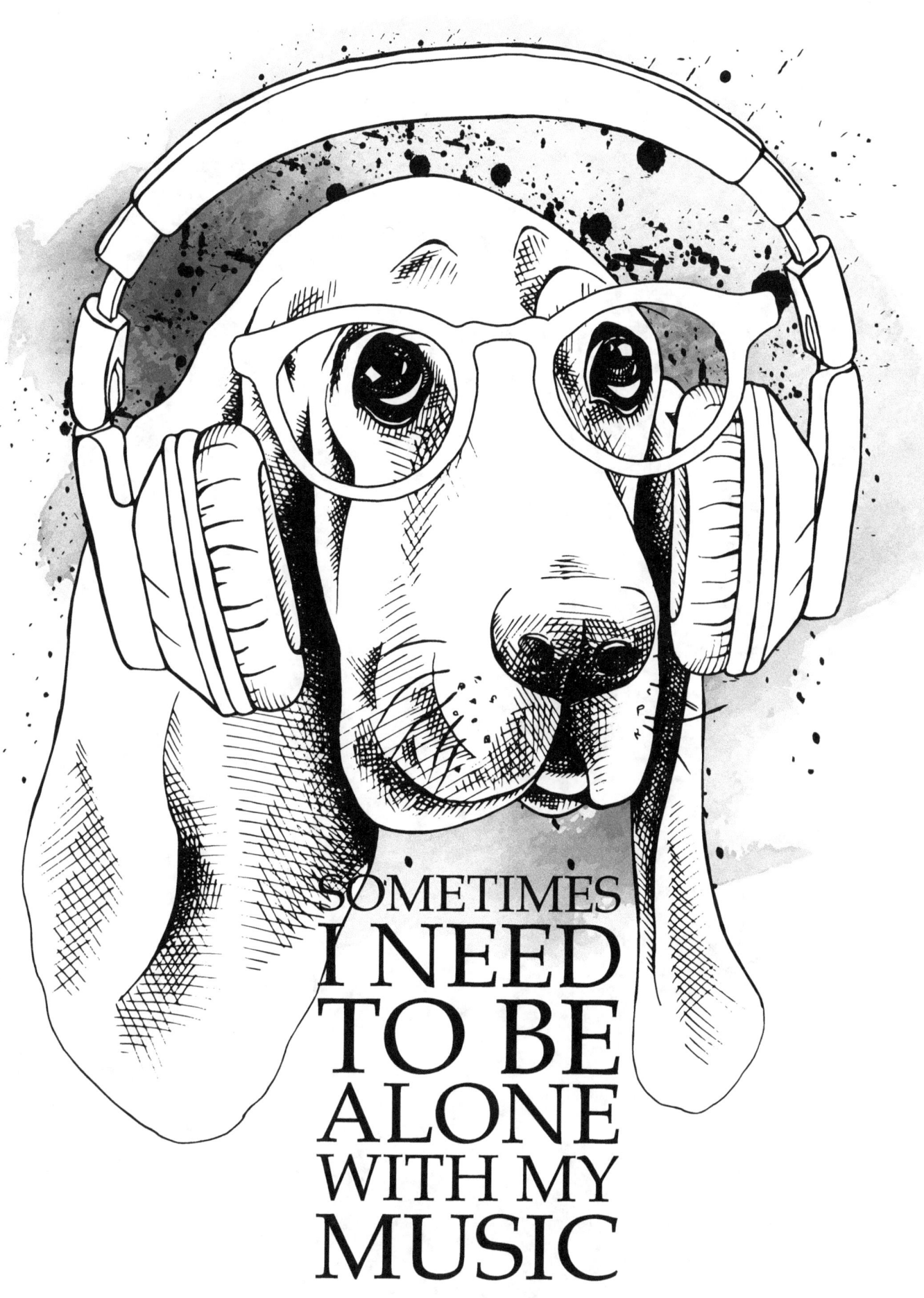

SOMETIMES
I NEED
TO BE
ALONE
WITH MY
MUSIC

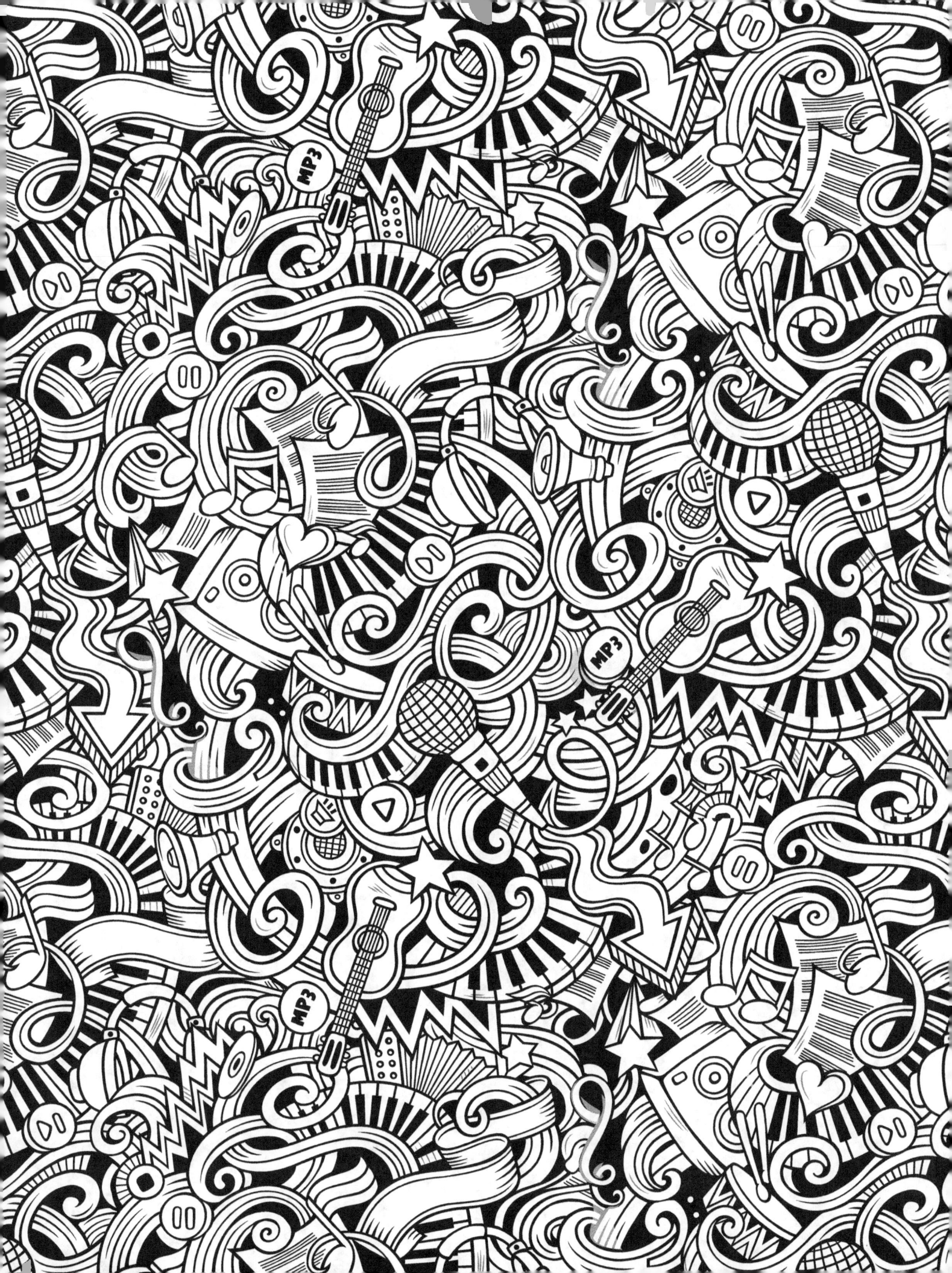

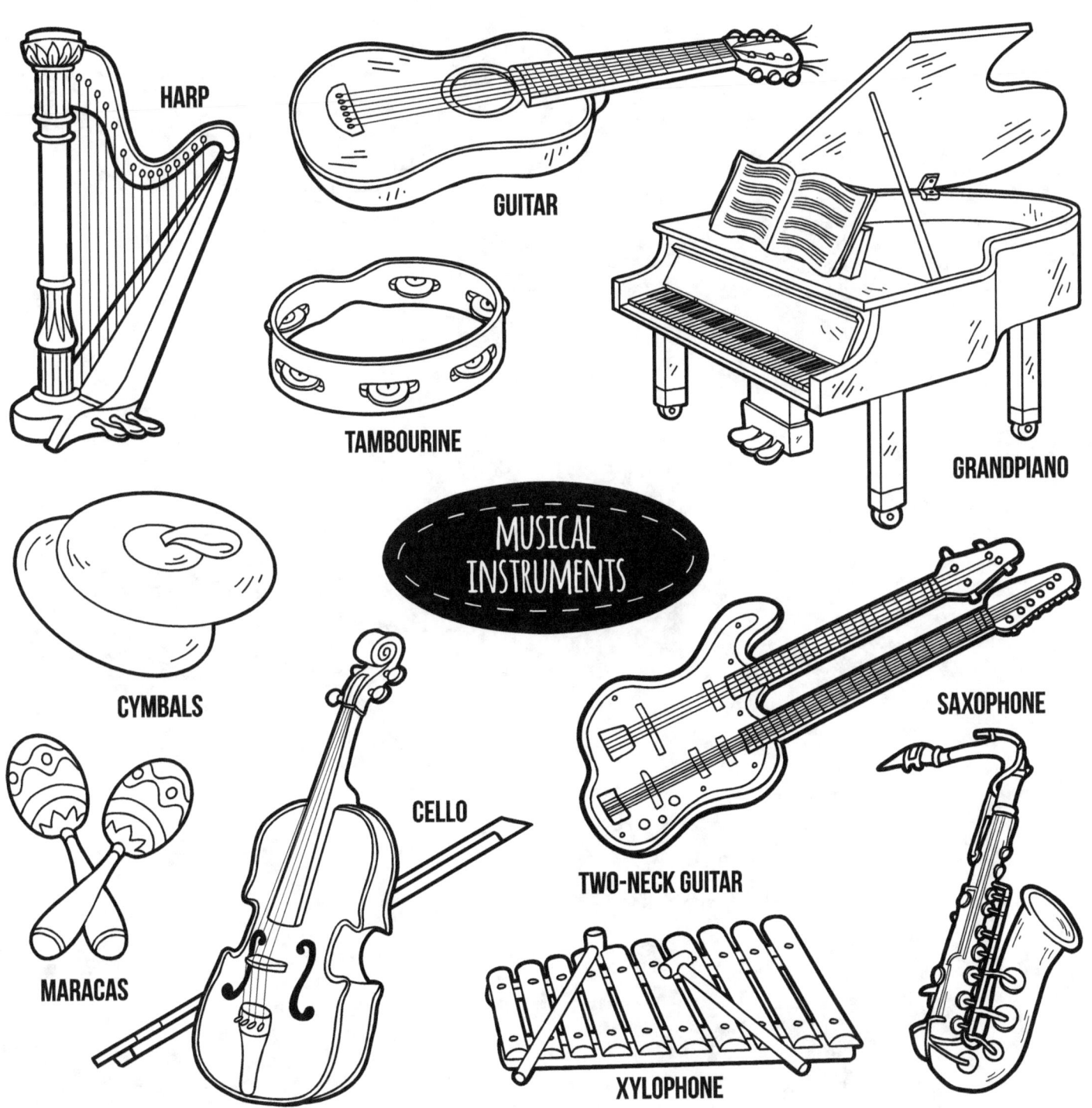

HARP

GUITAR

GRANDPIANO

TAMBOURINE

MUSICAL INSTRUMENTS

CYMBALS

SAXOPHONE

CELLO

MARACAS

TWO-NECK GUITAR

XYLOPHONE

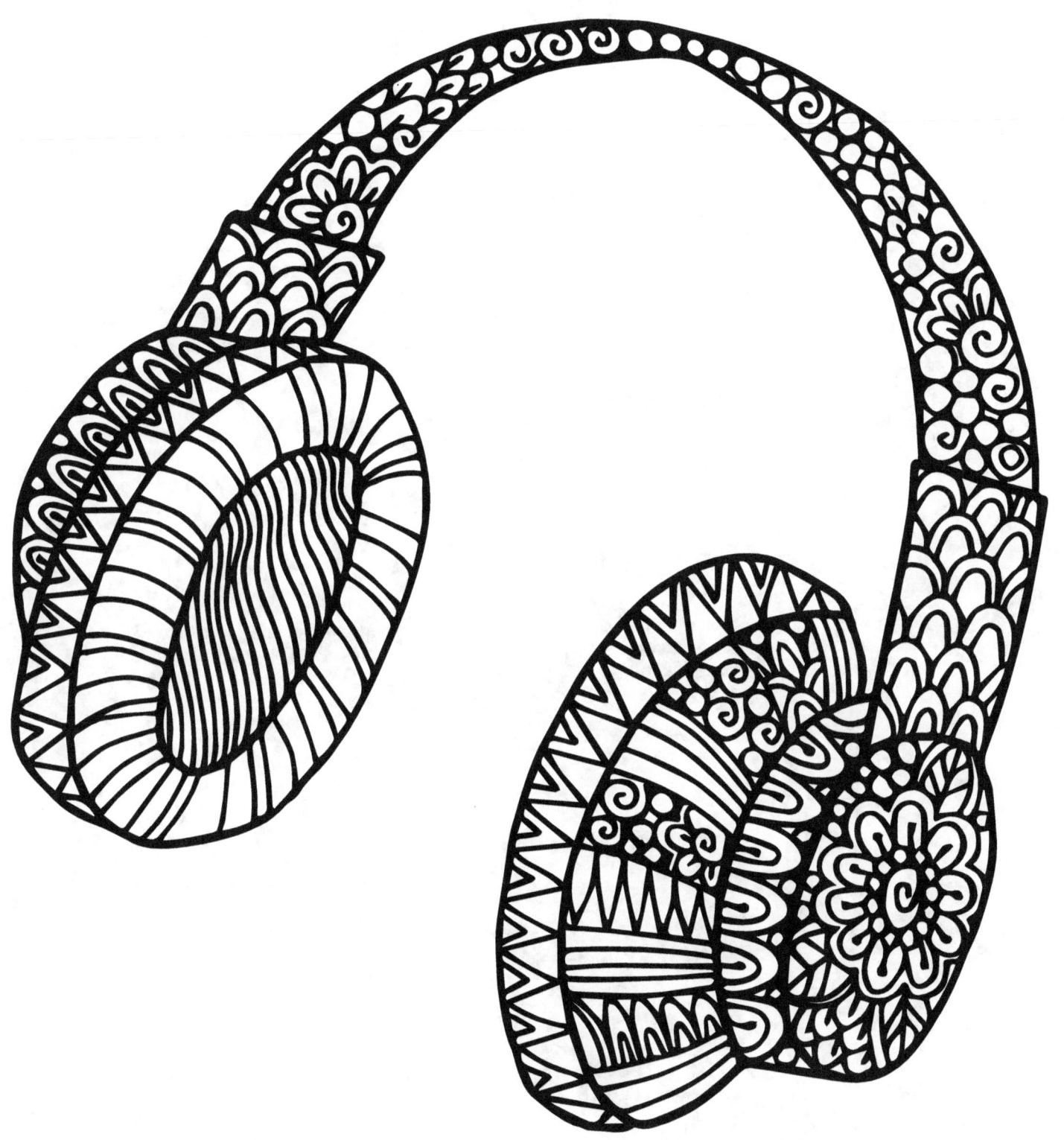

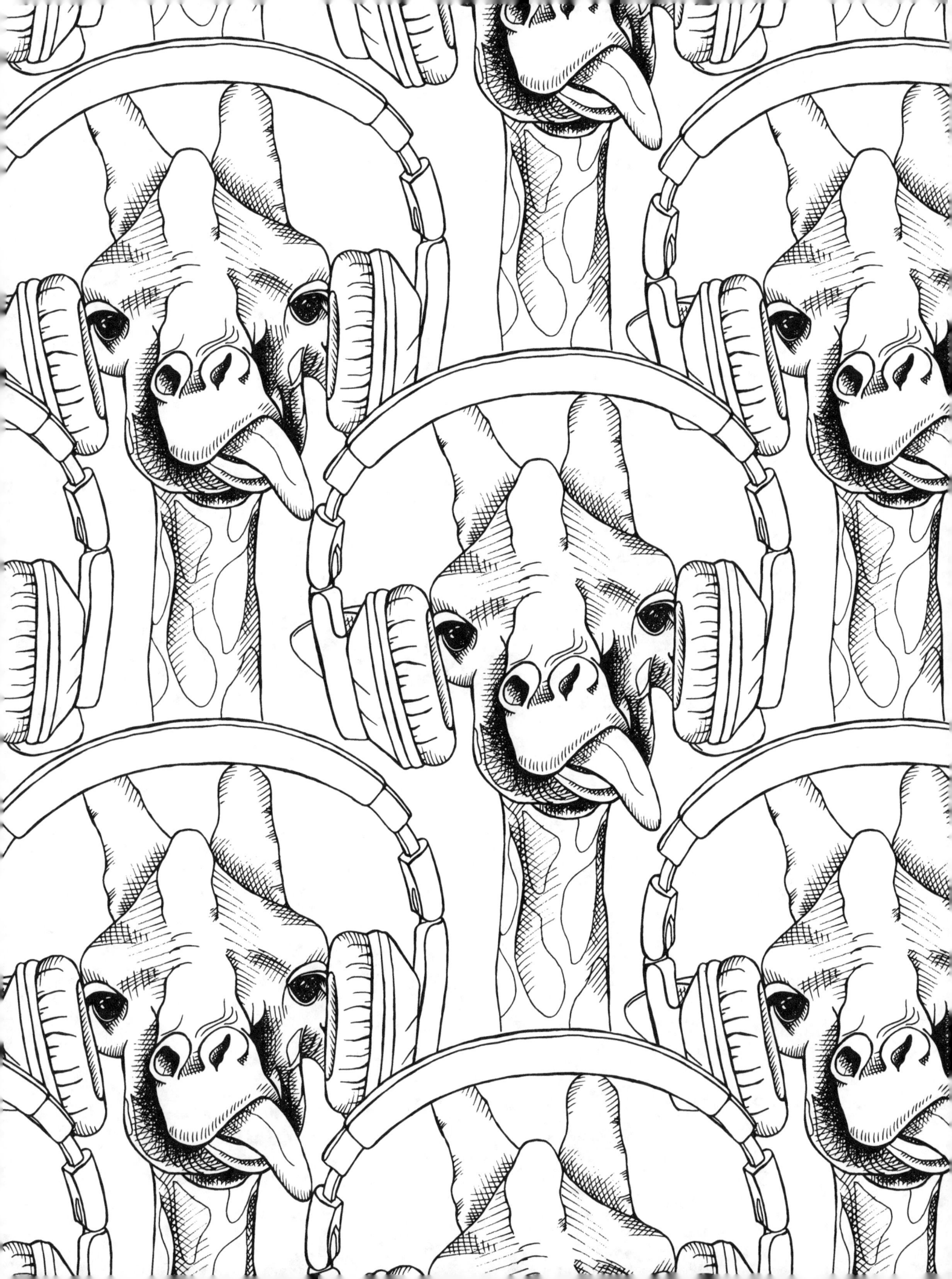

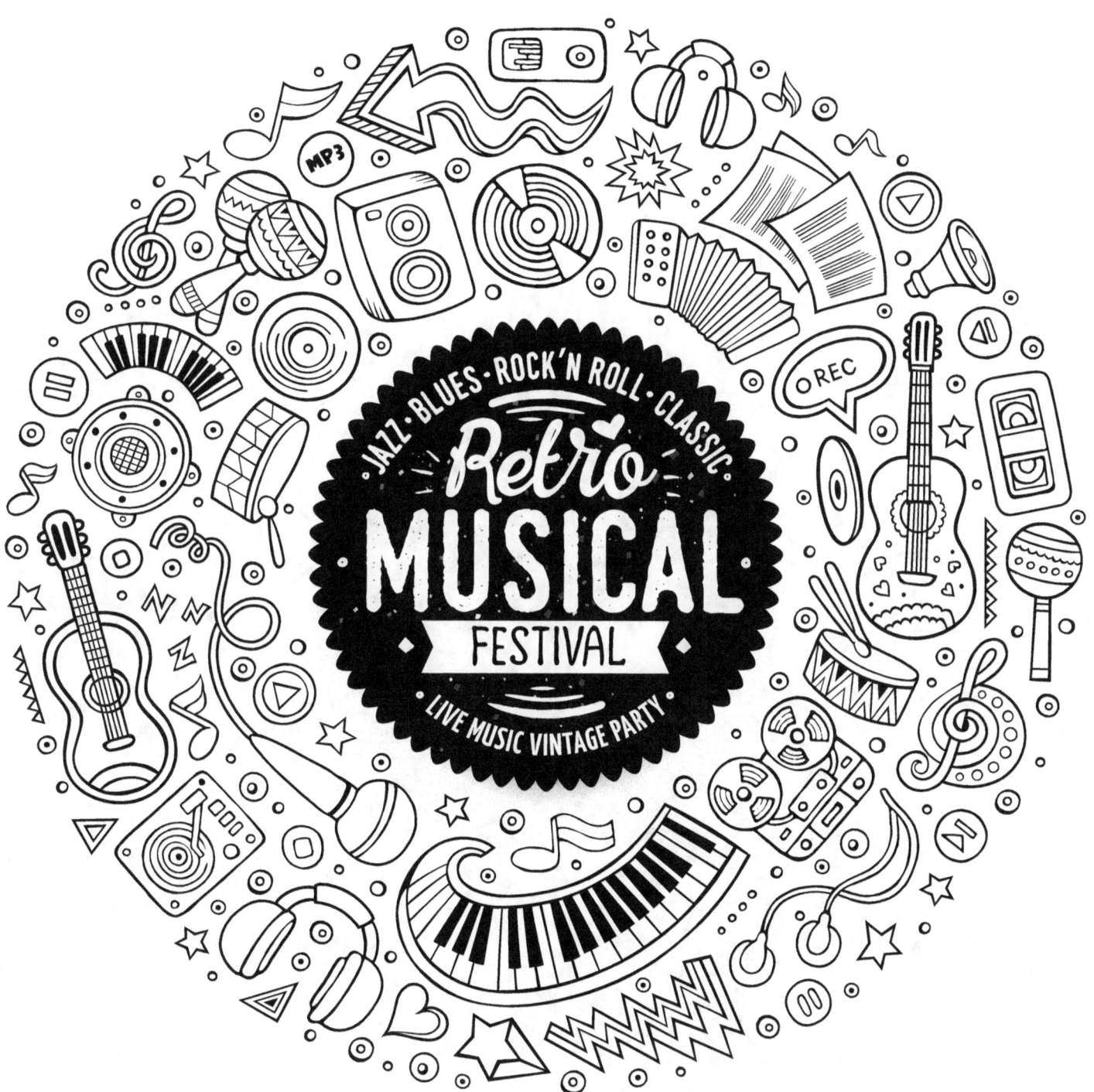

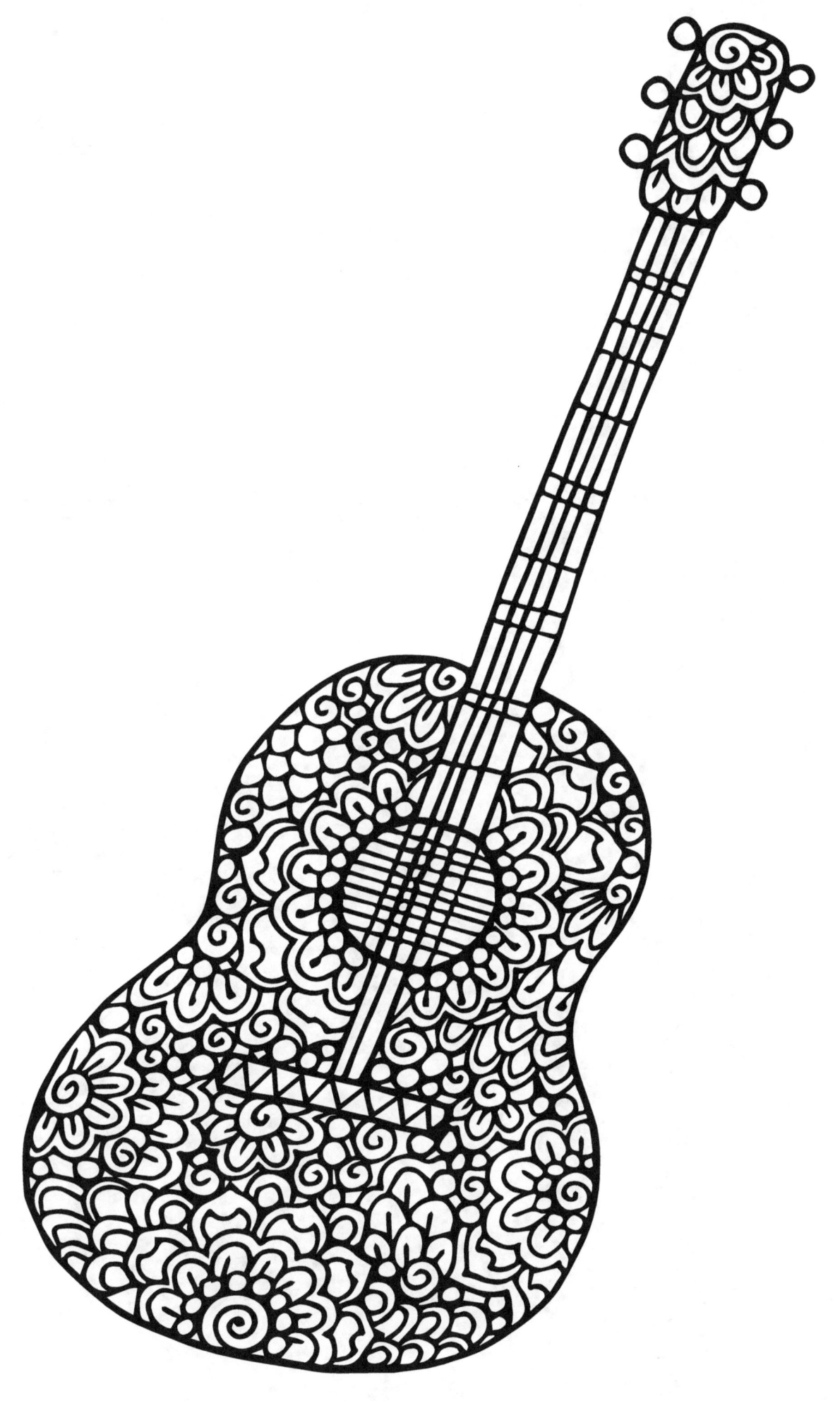

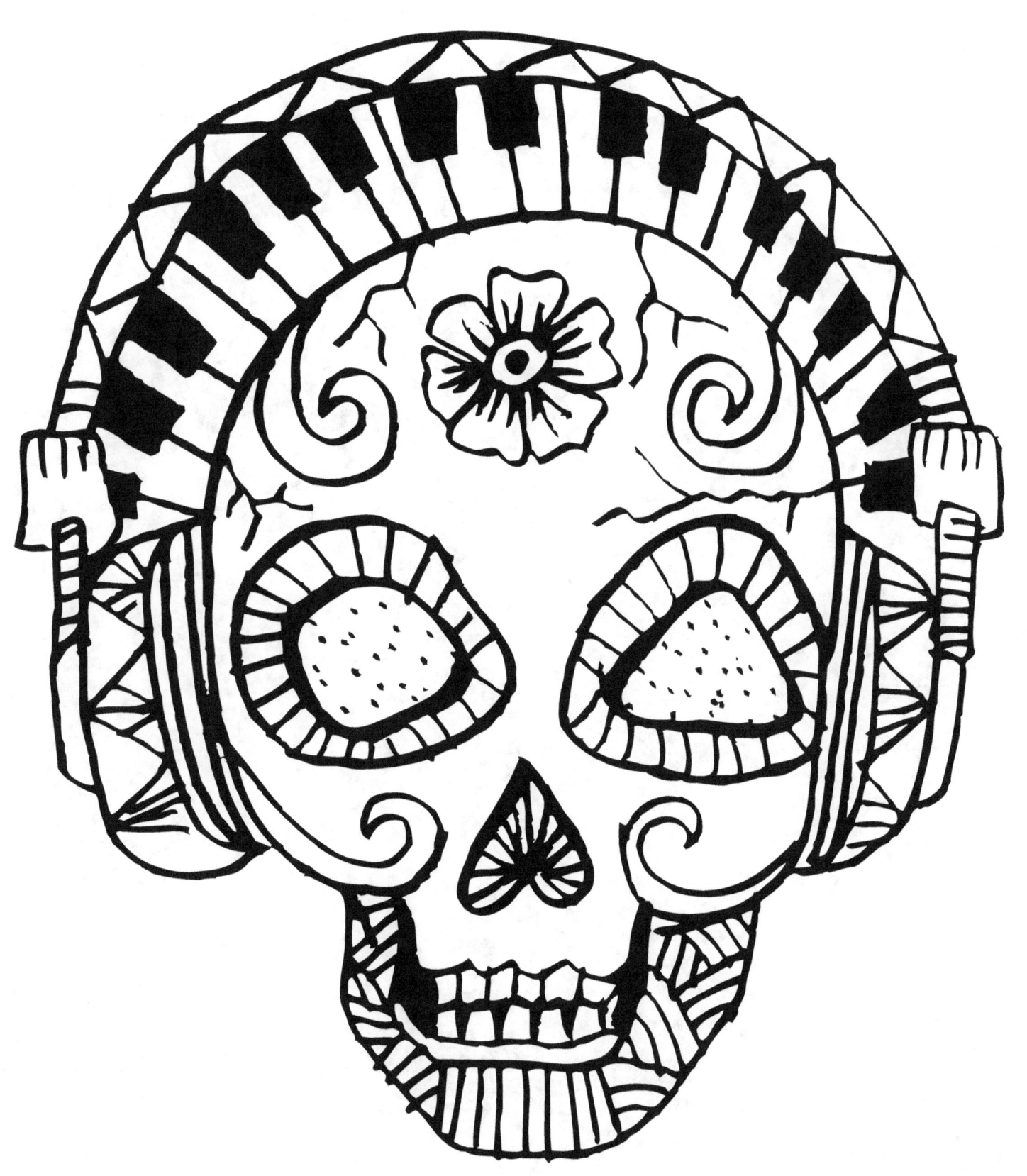

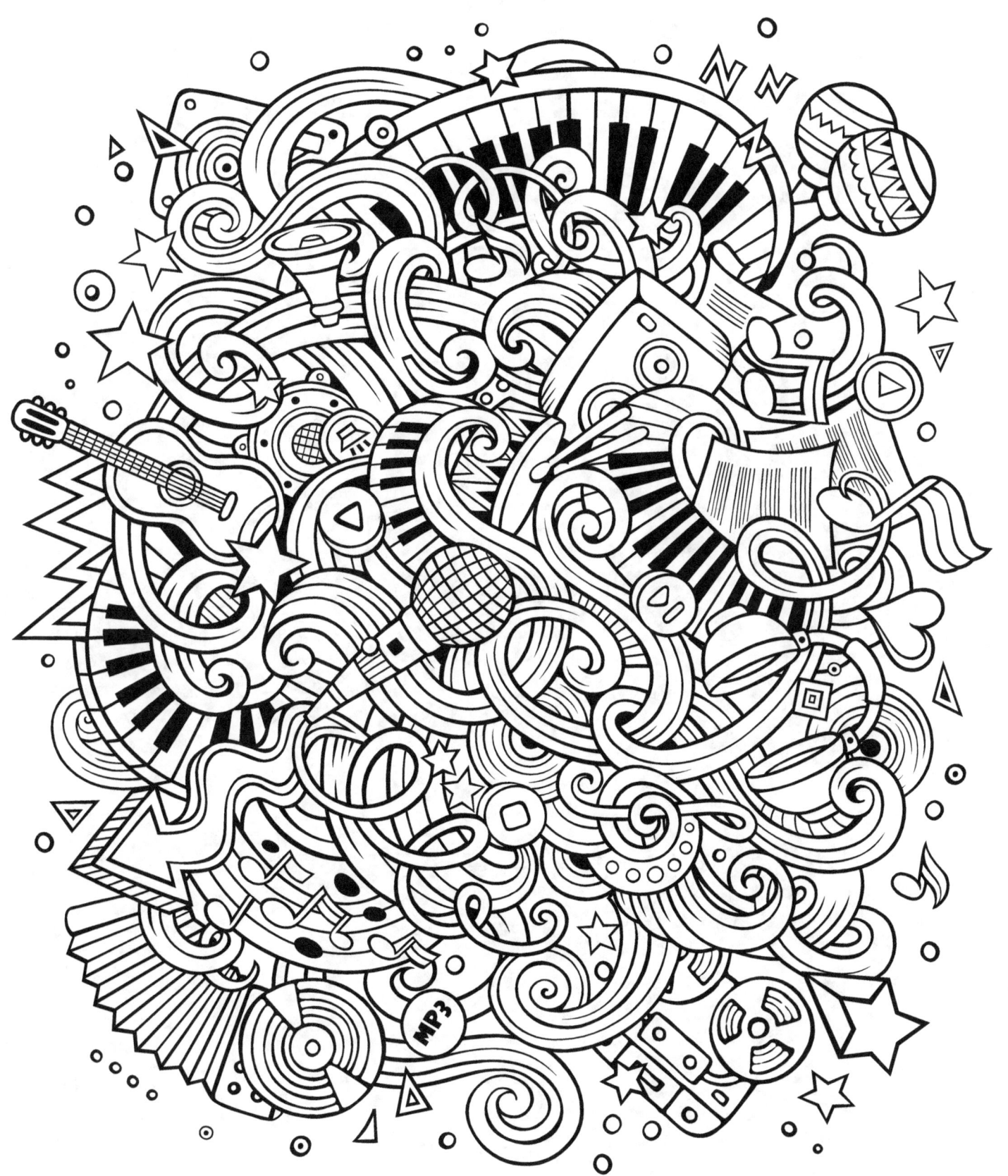

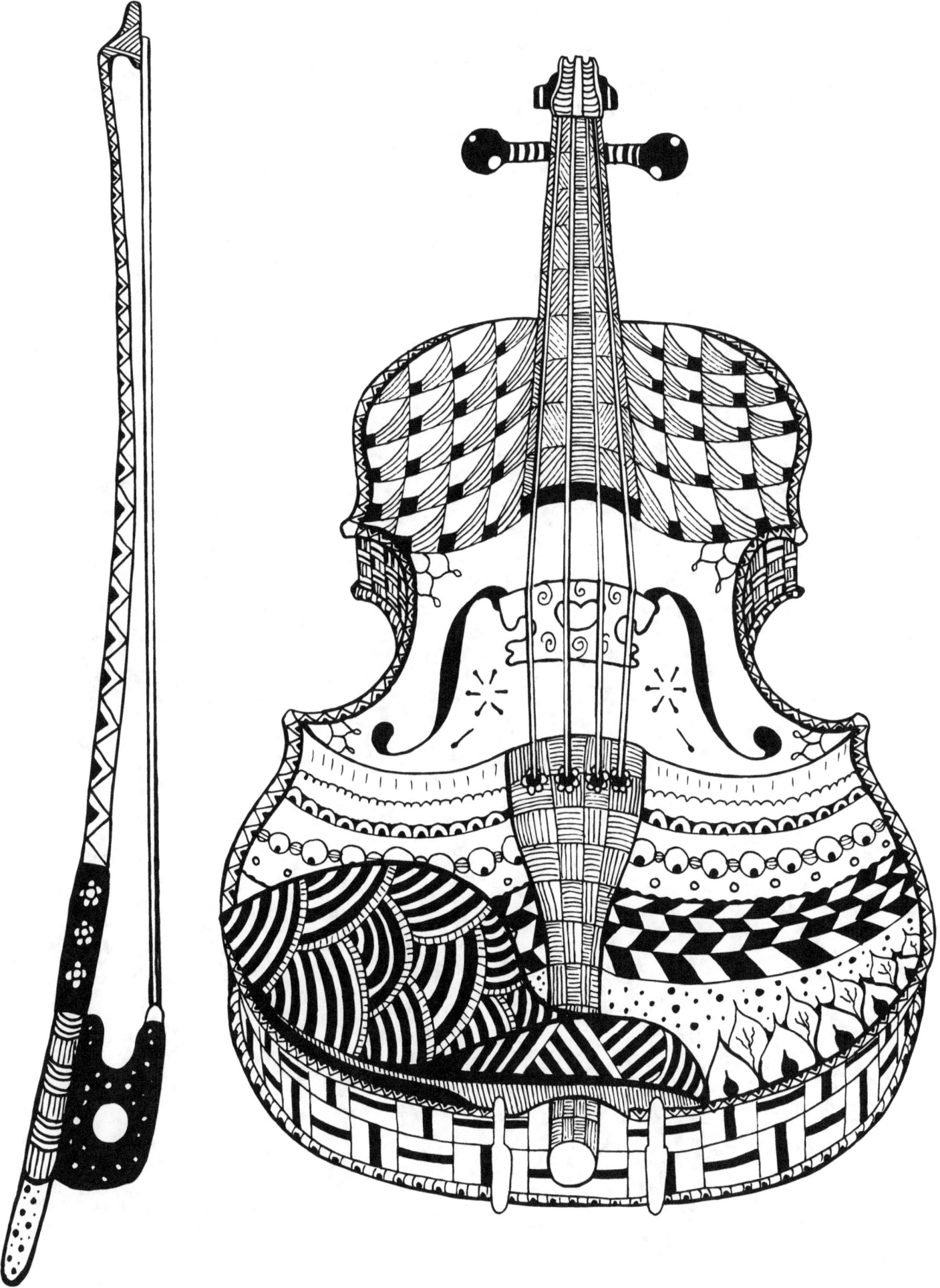

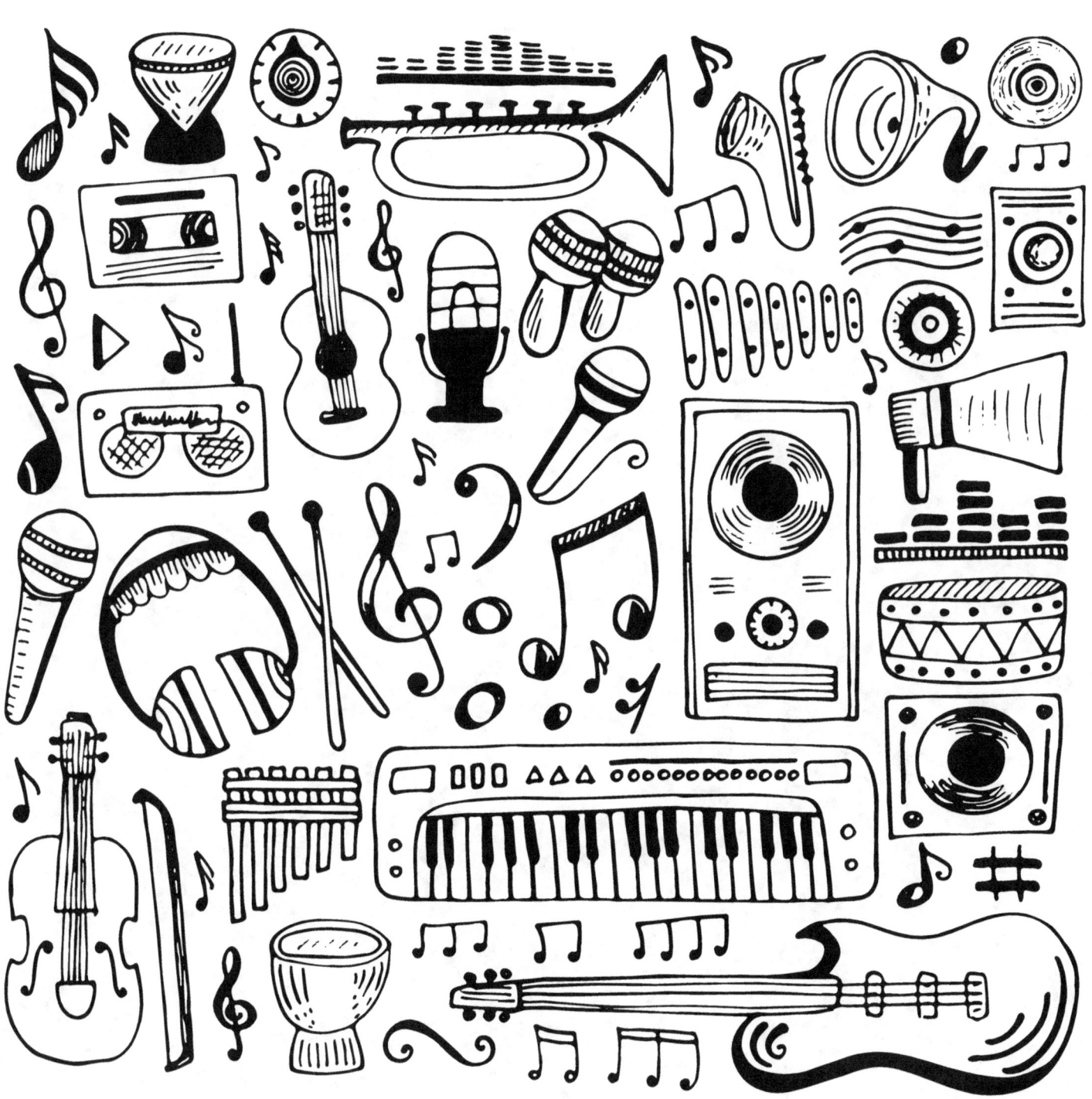

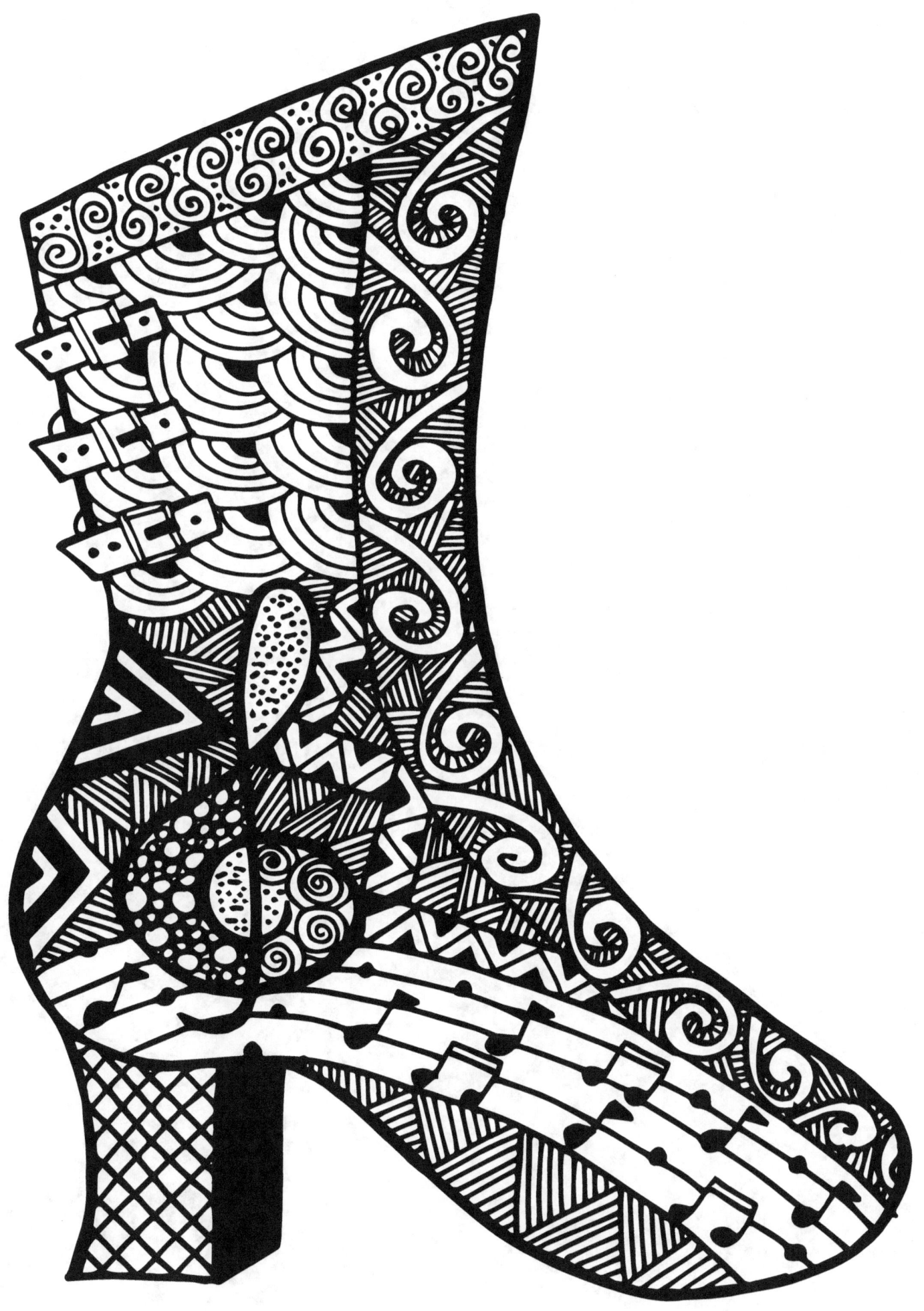

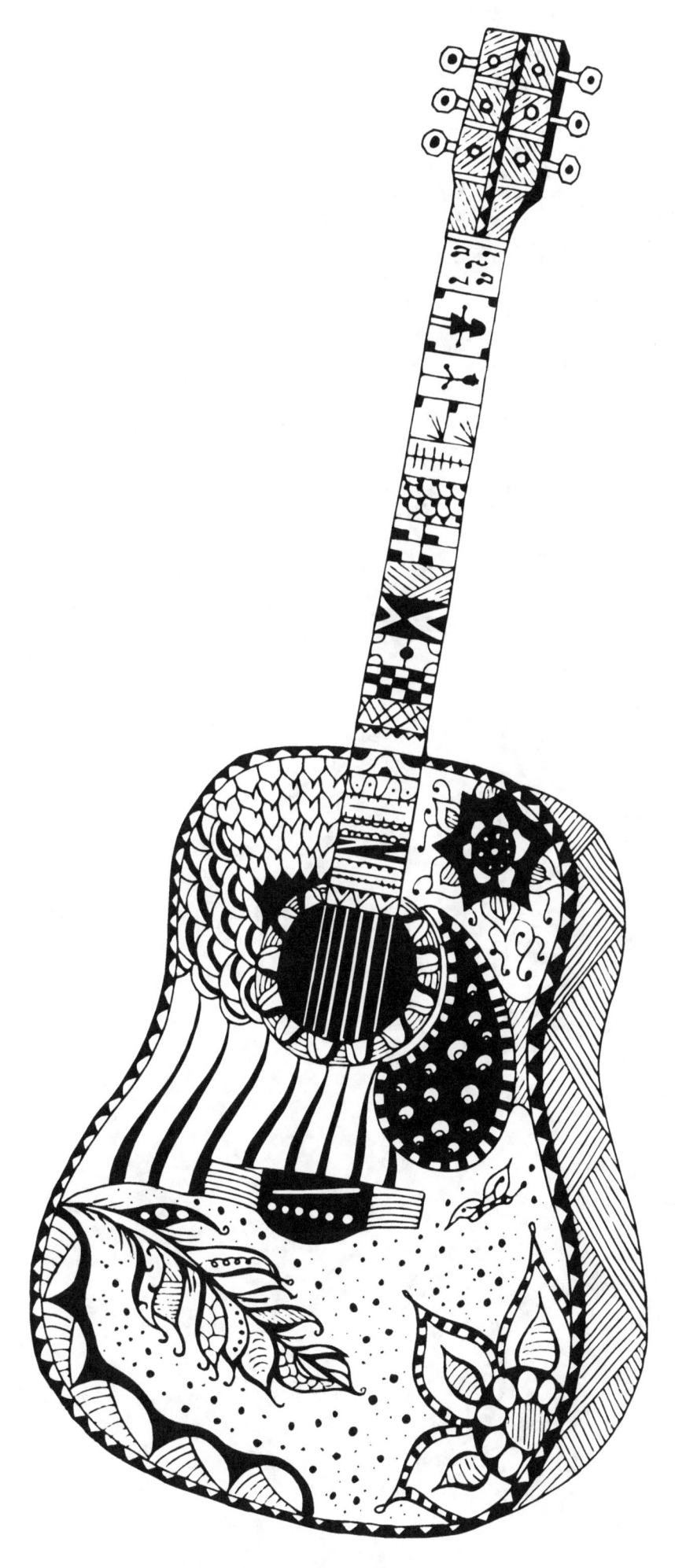

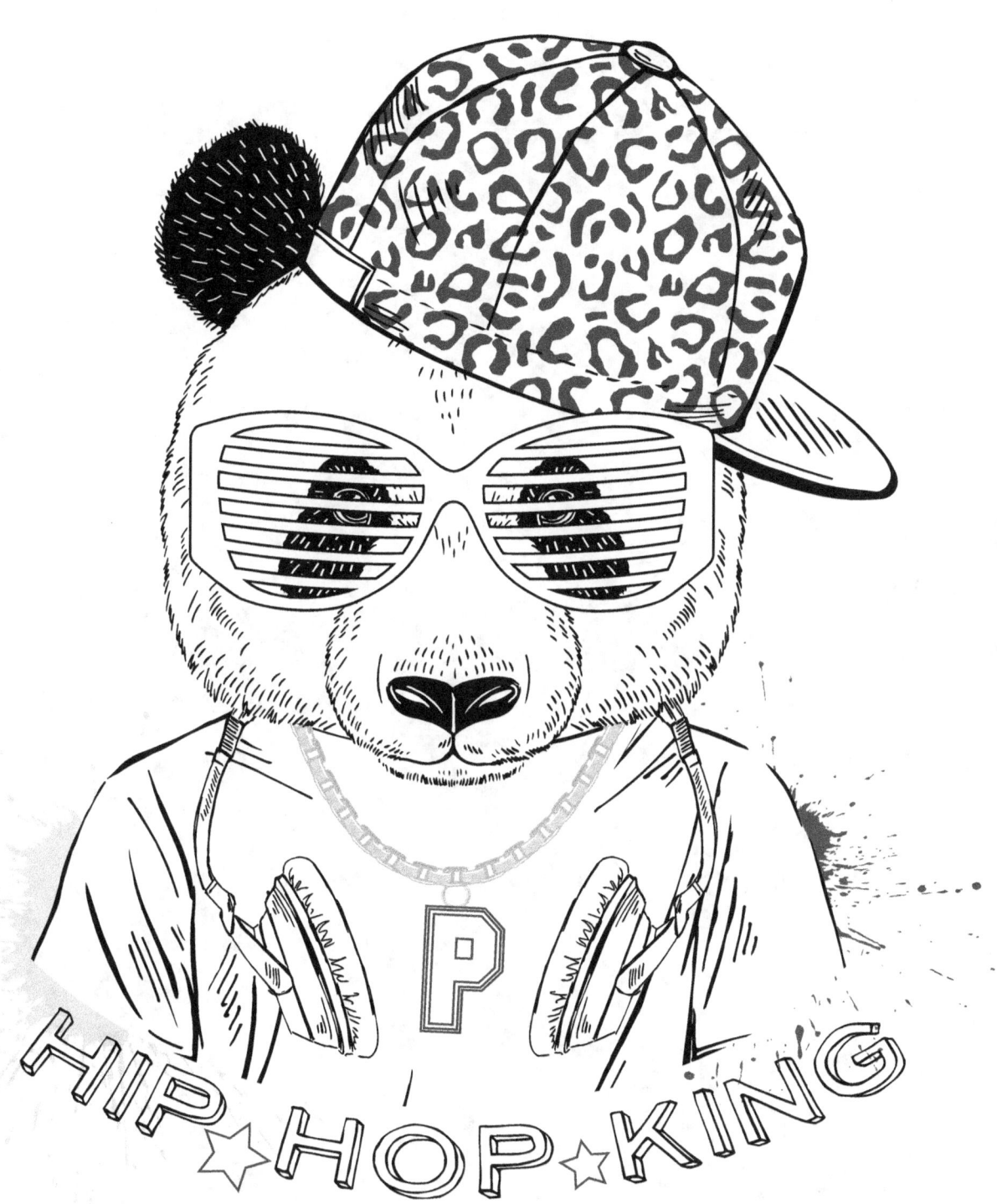

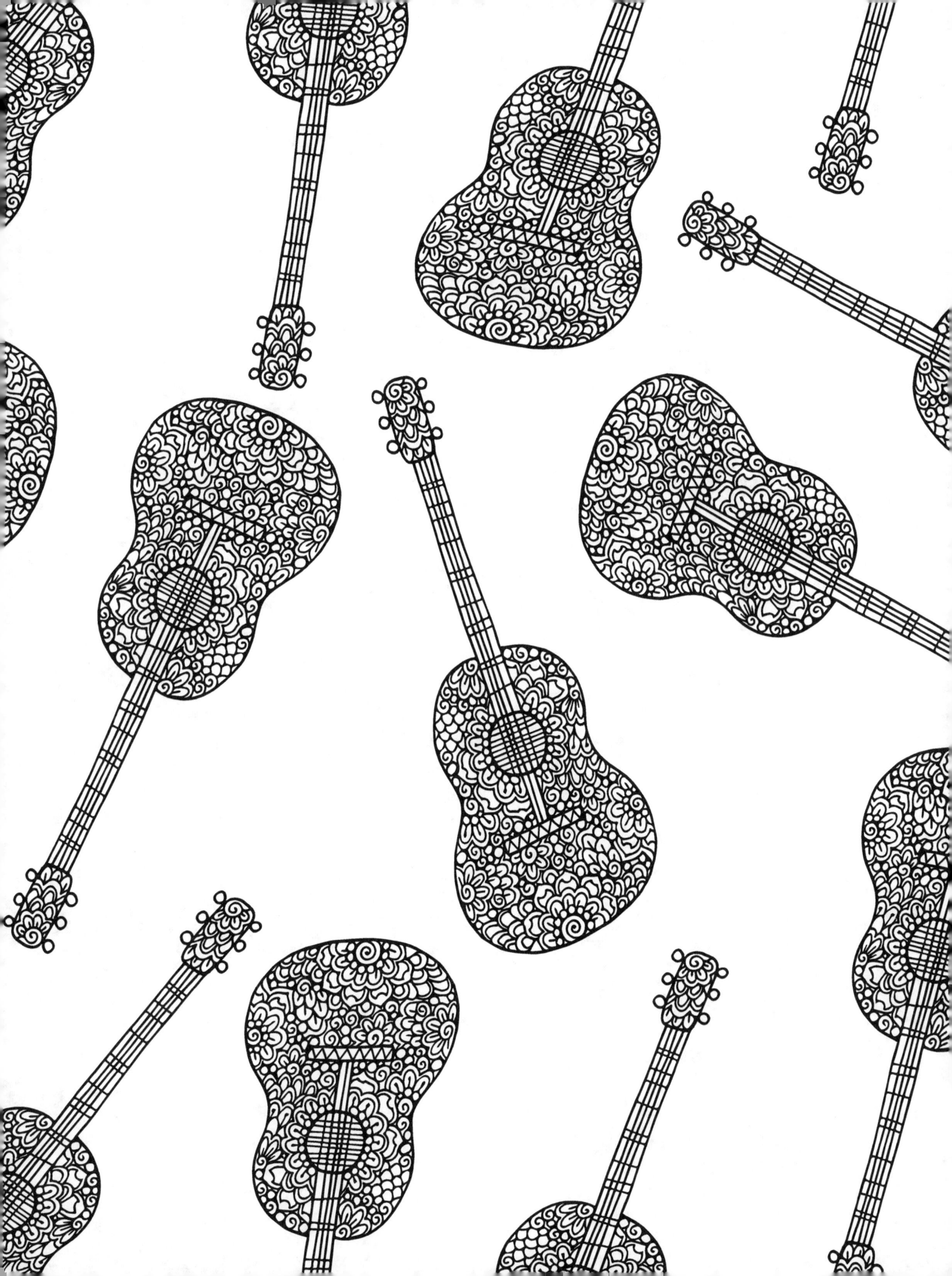

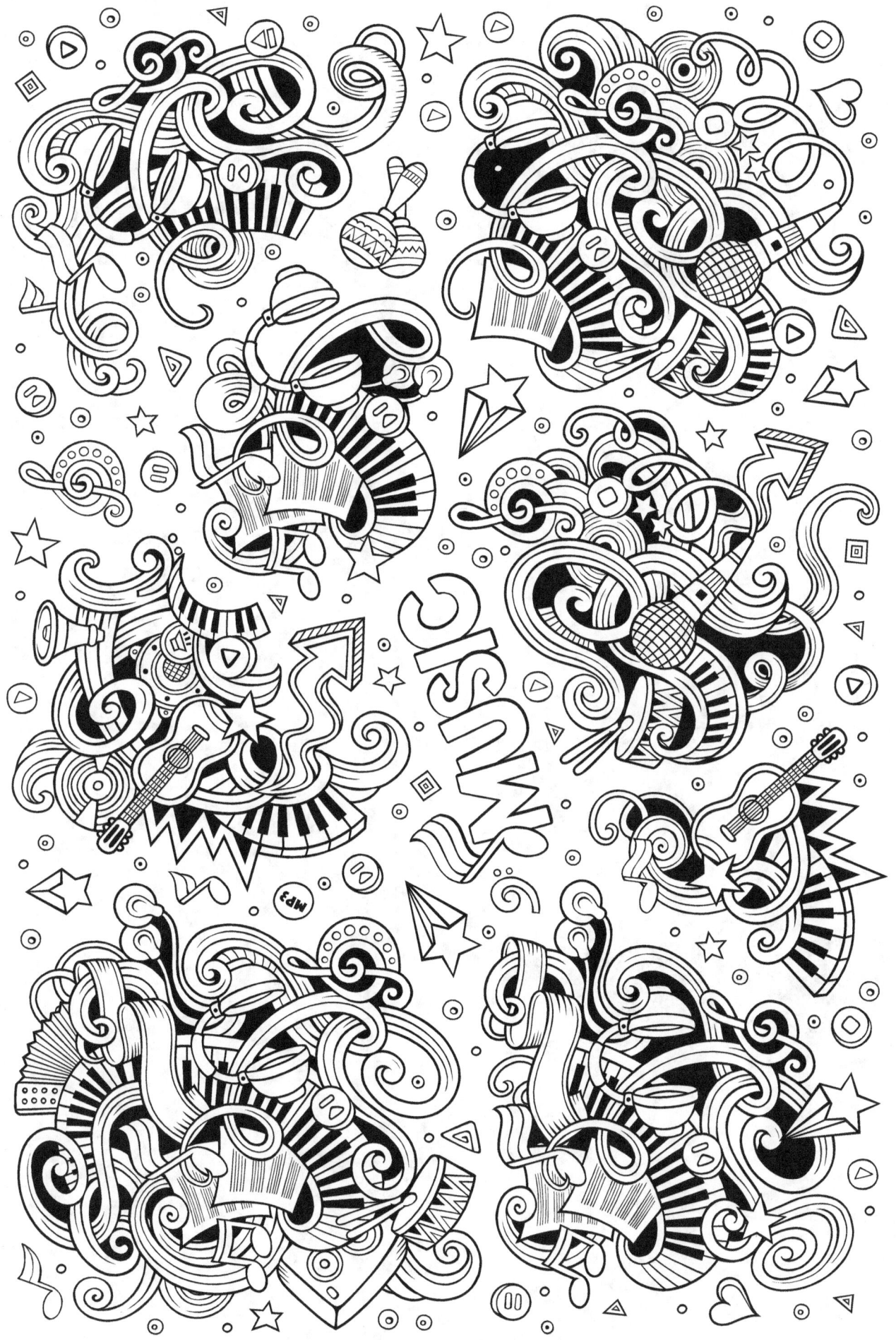

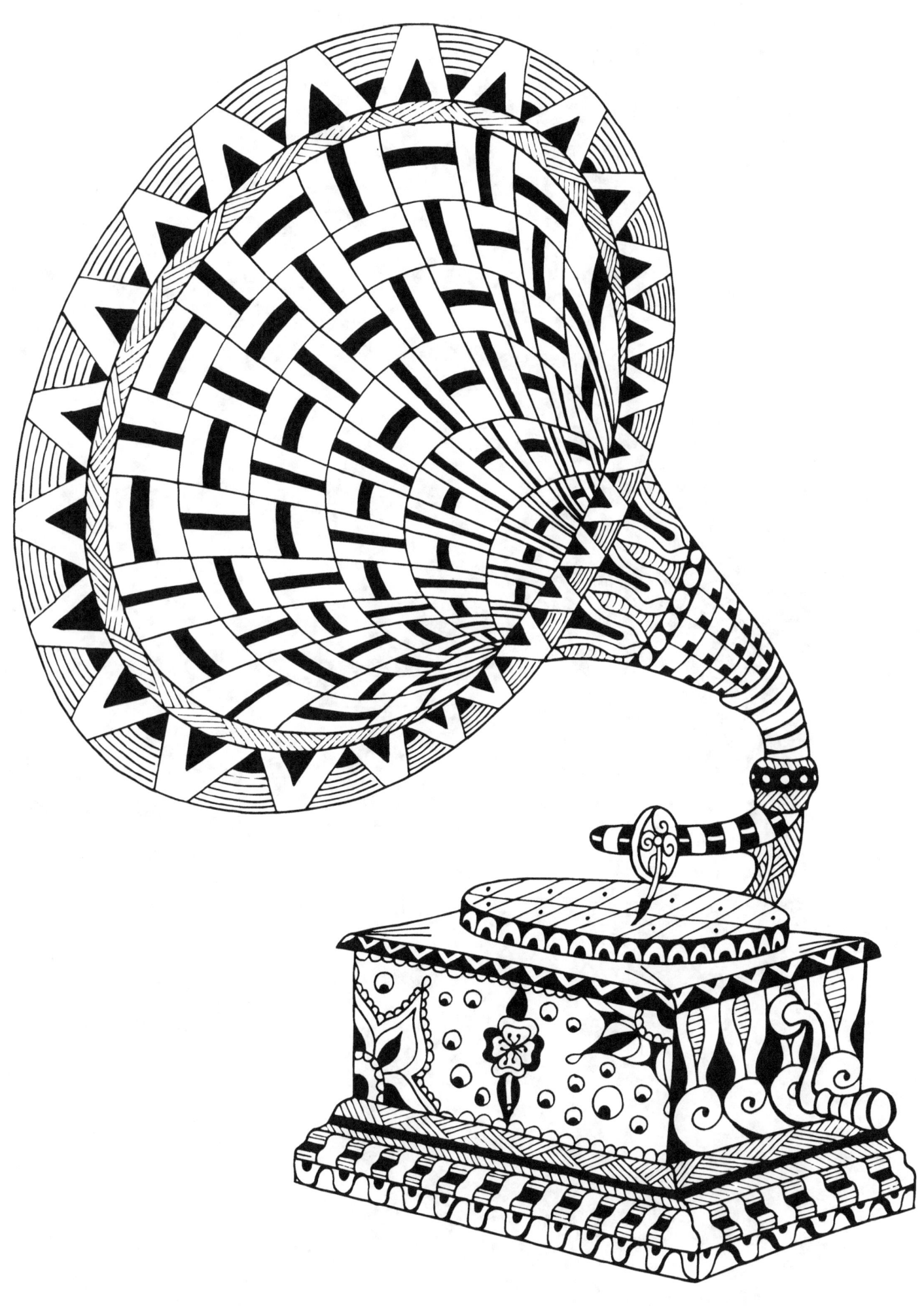

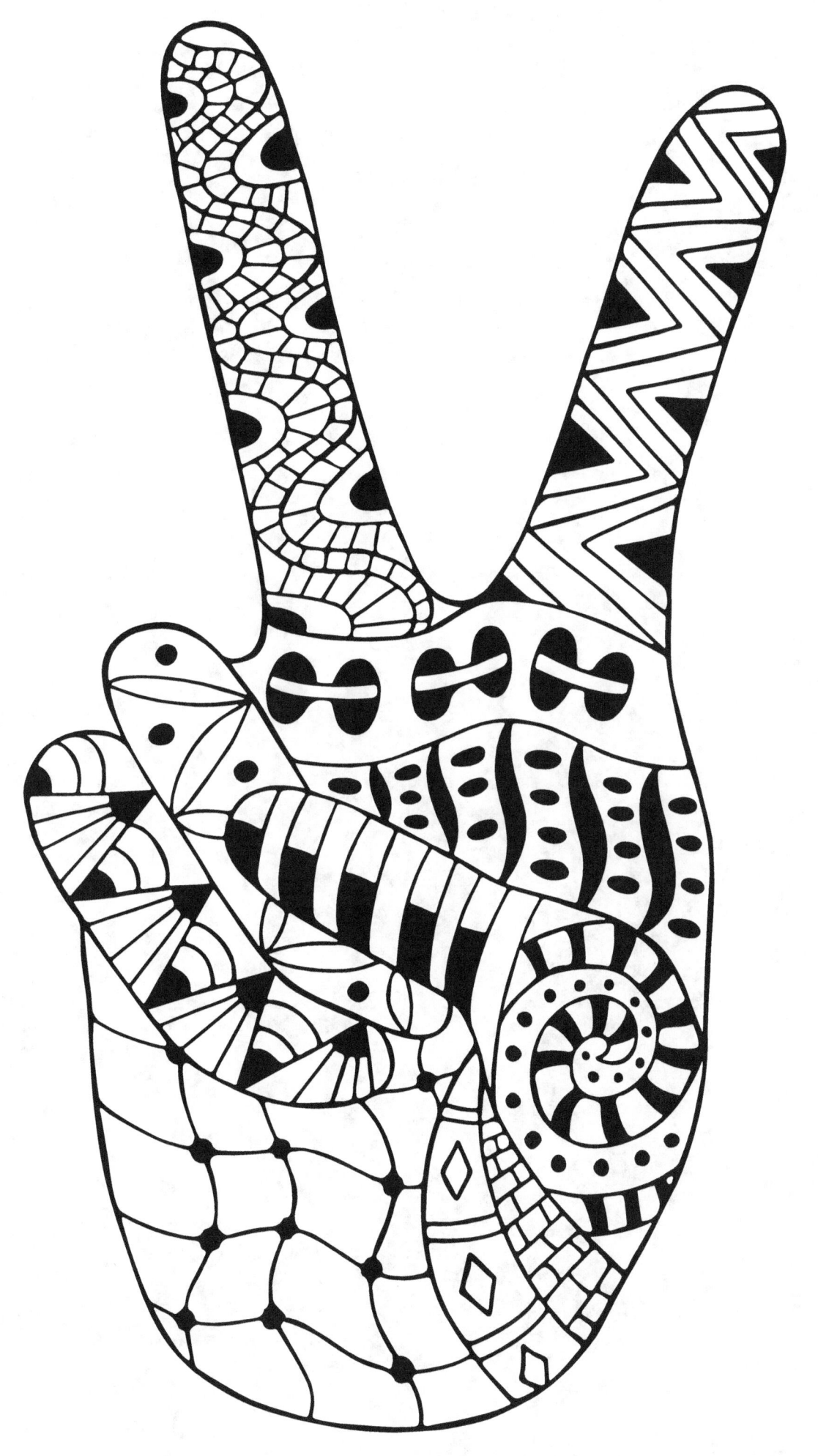

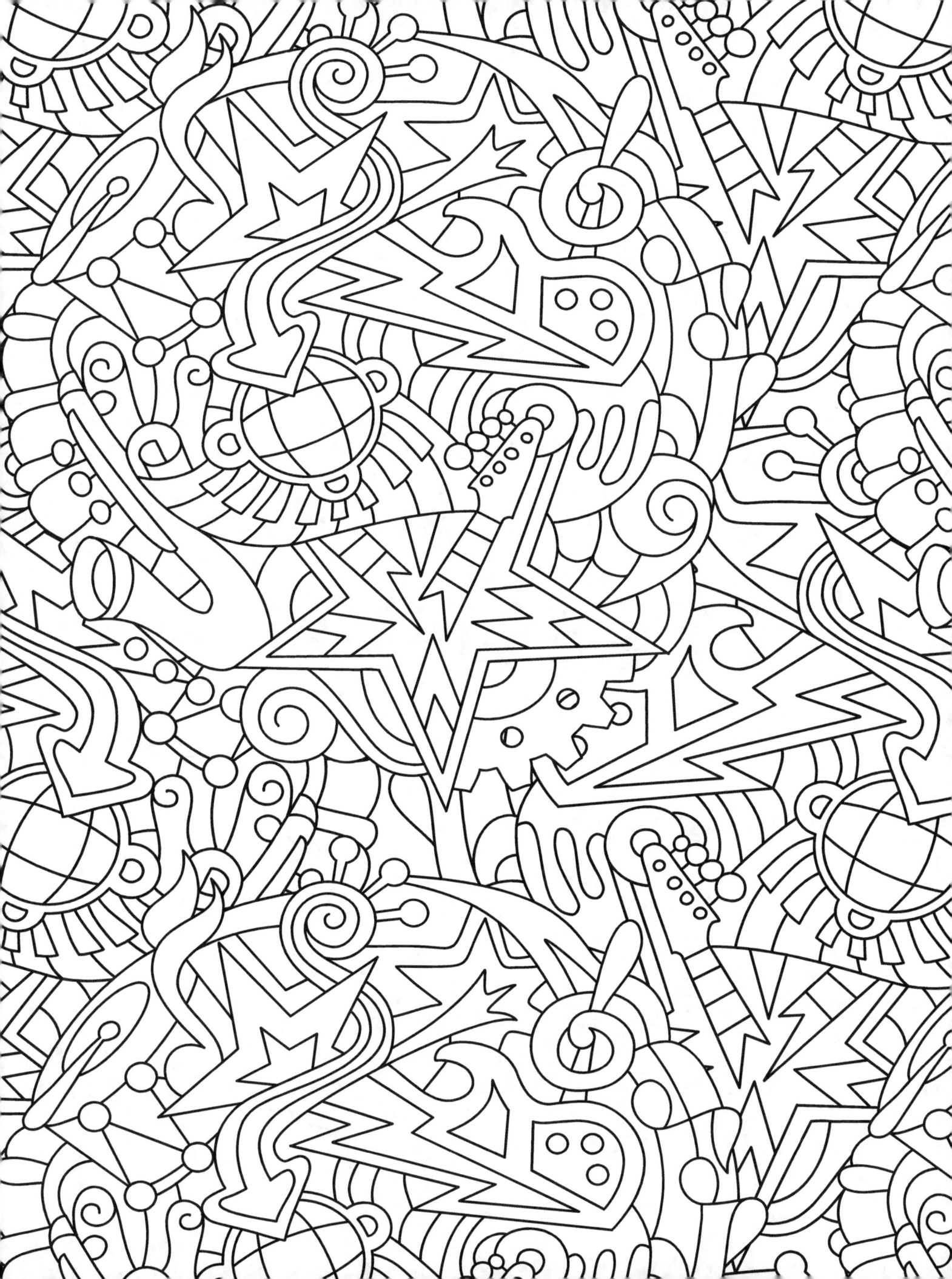

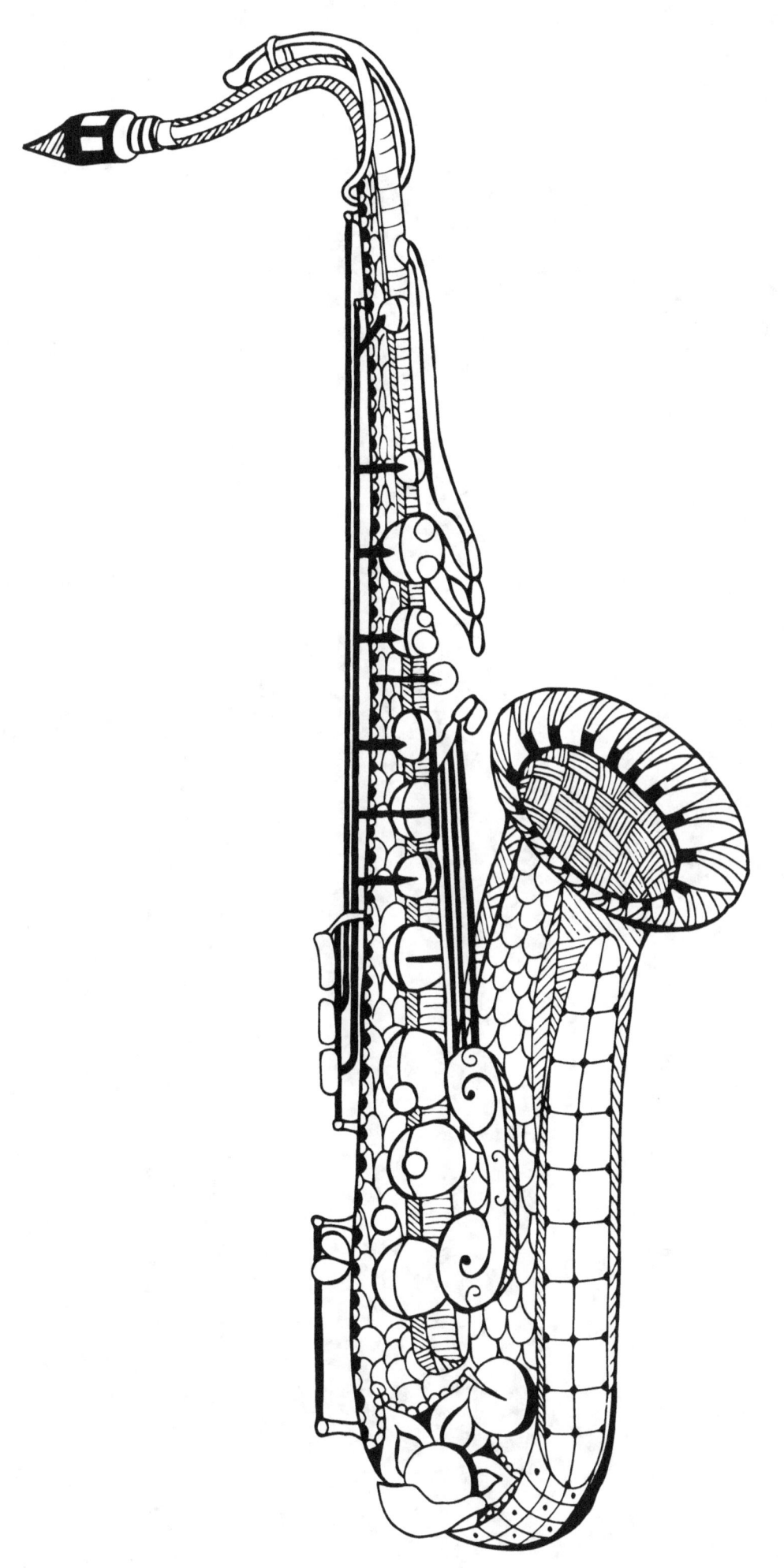

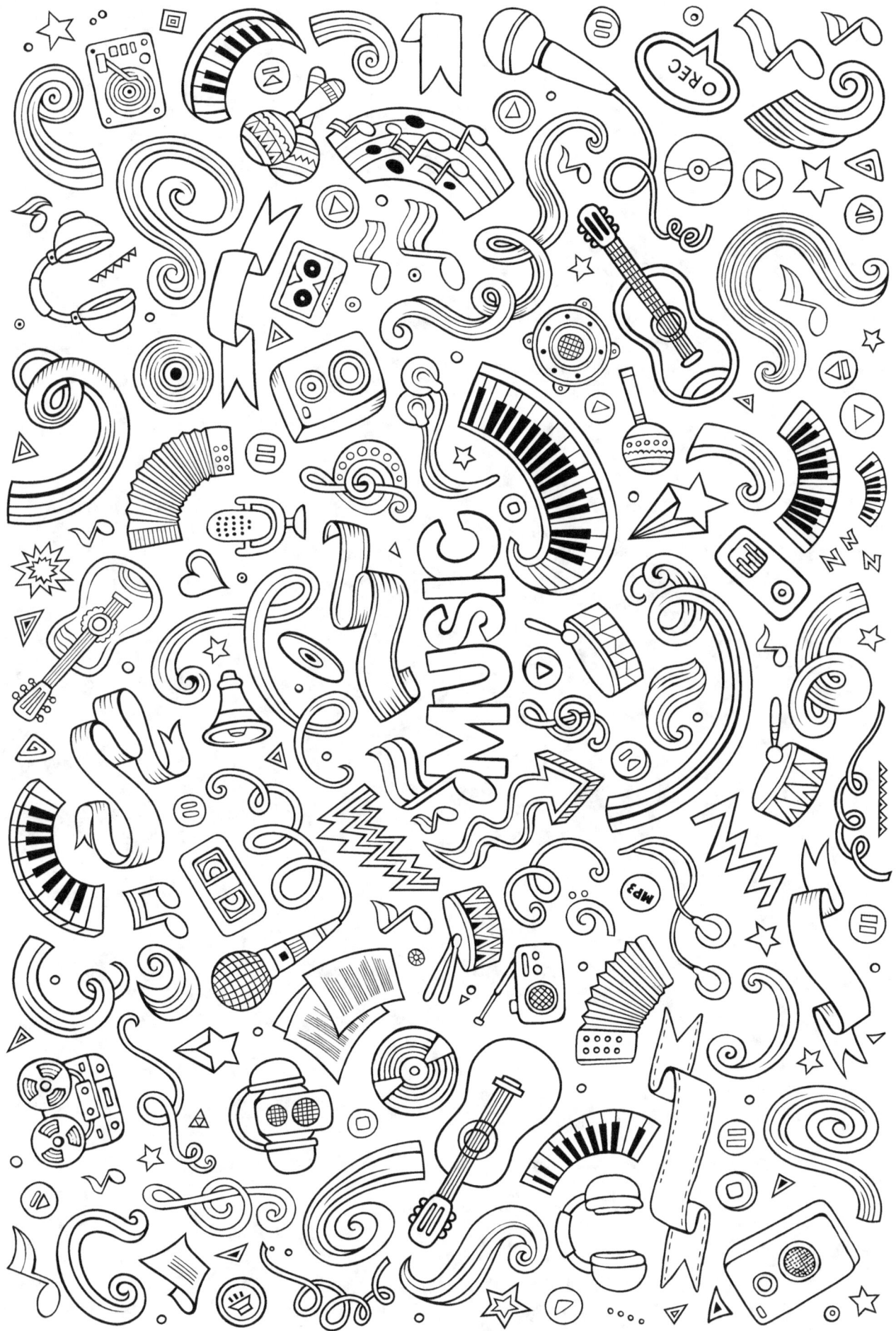

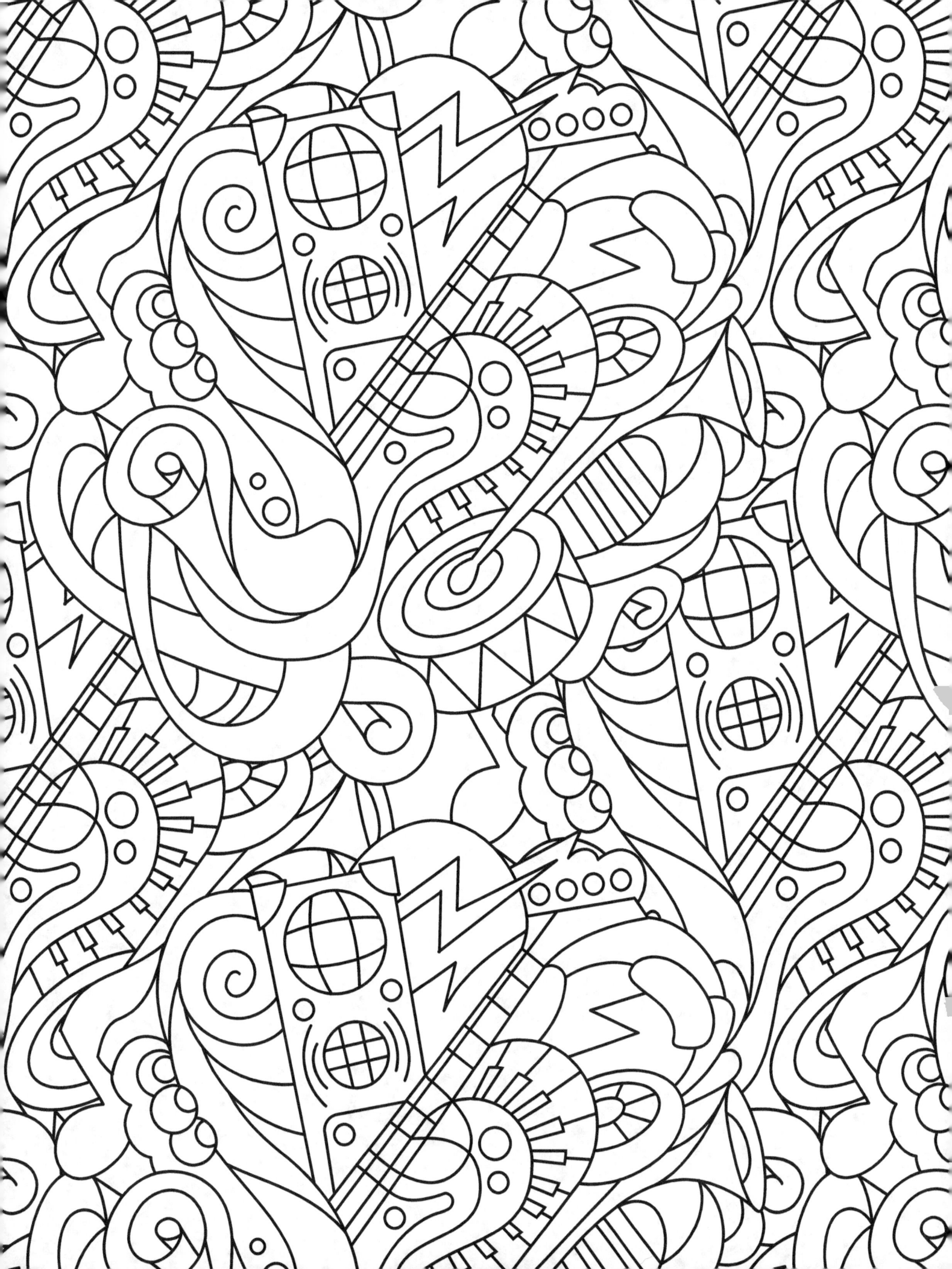

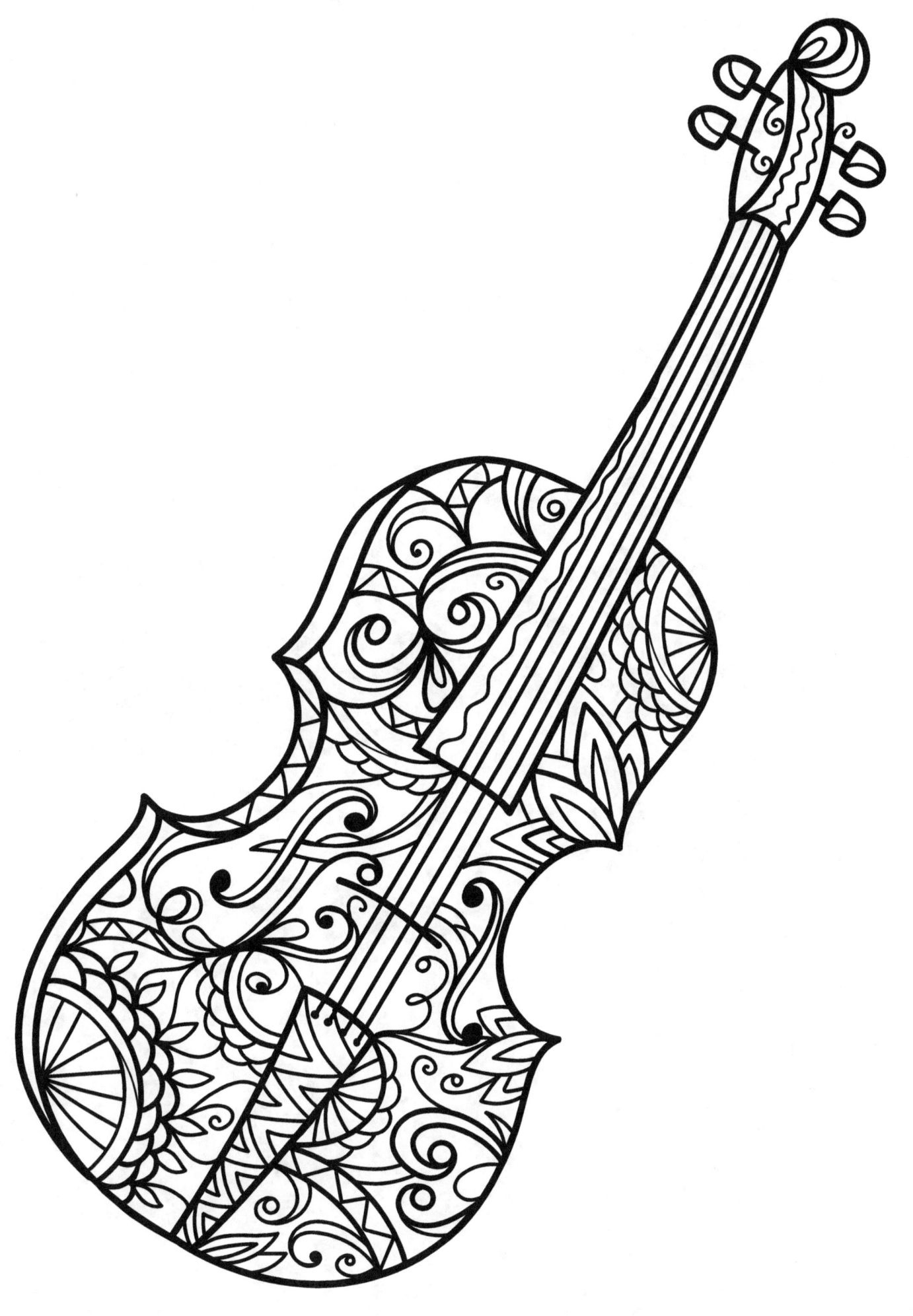

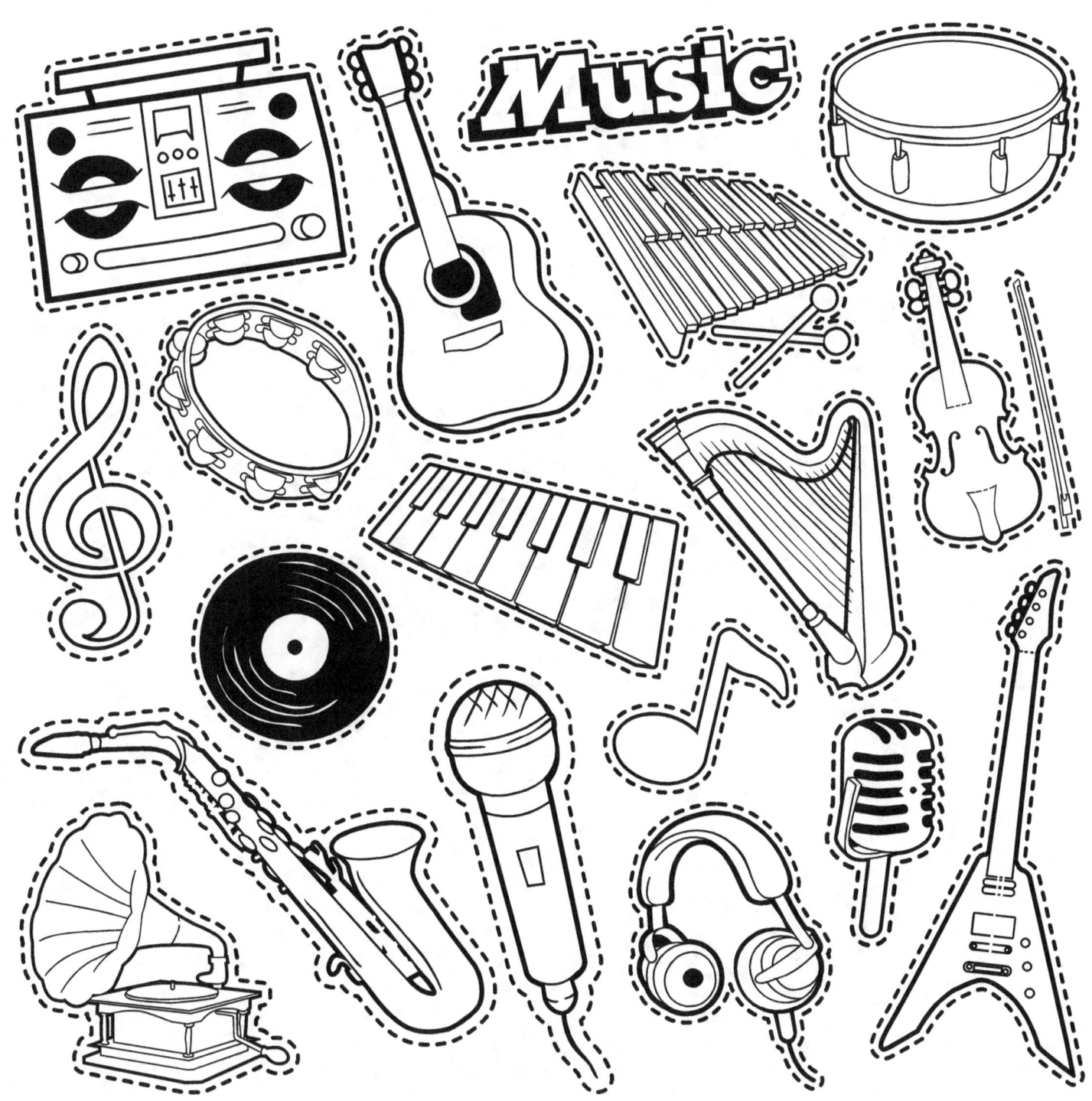

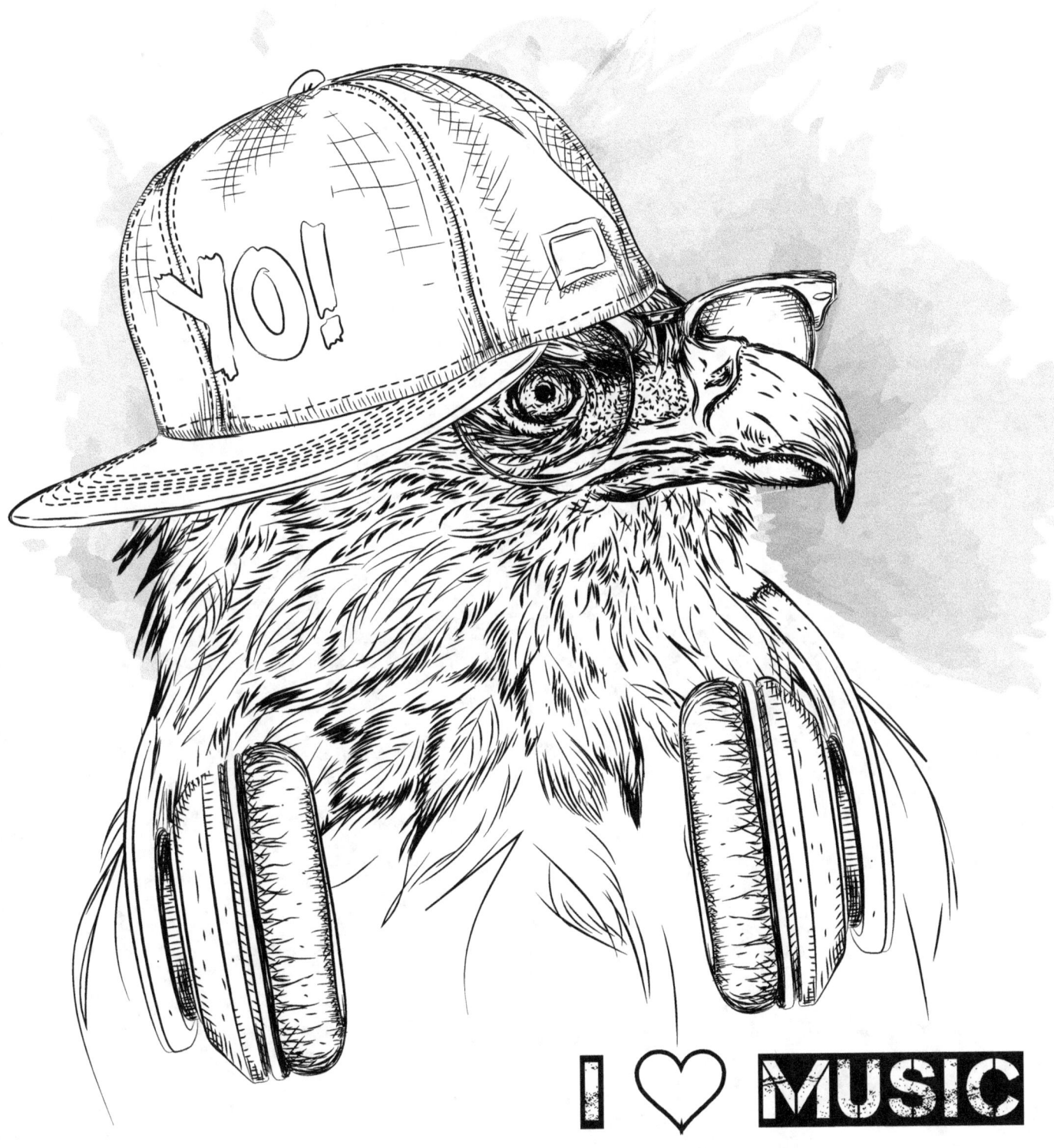

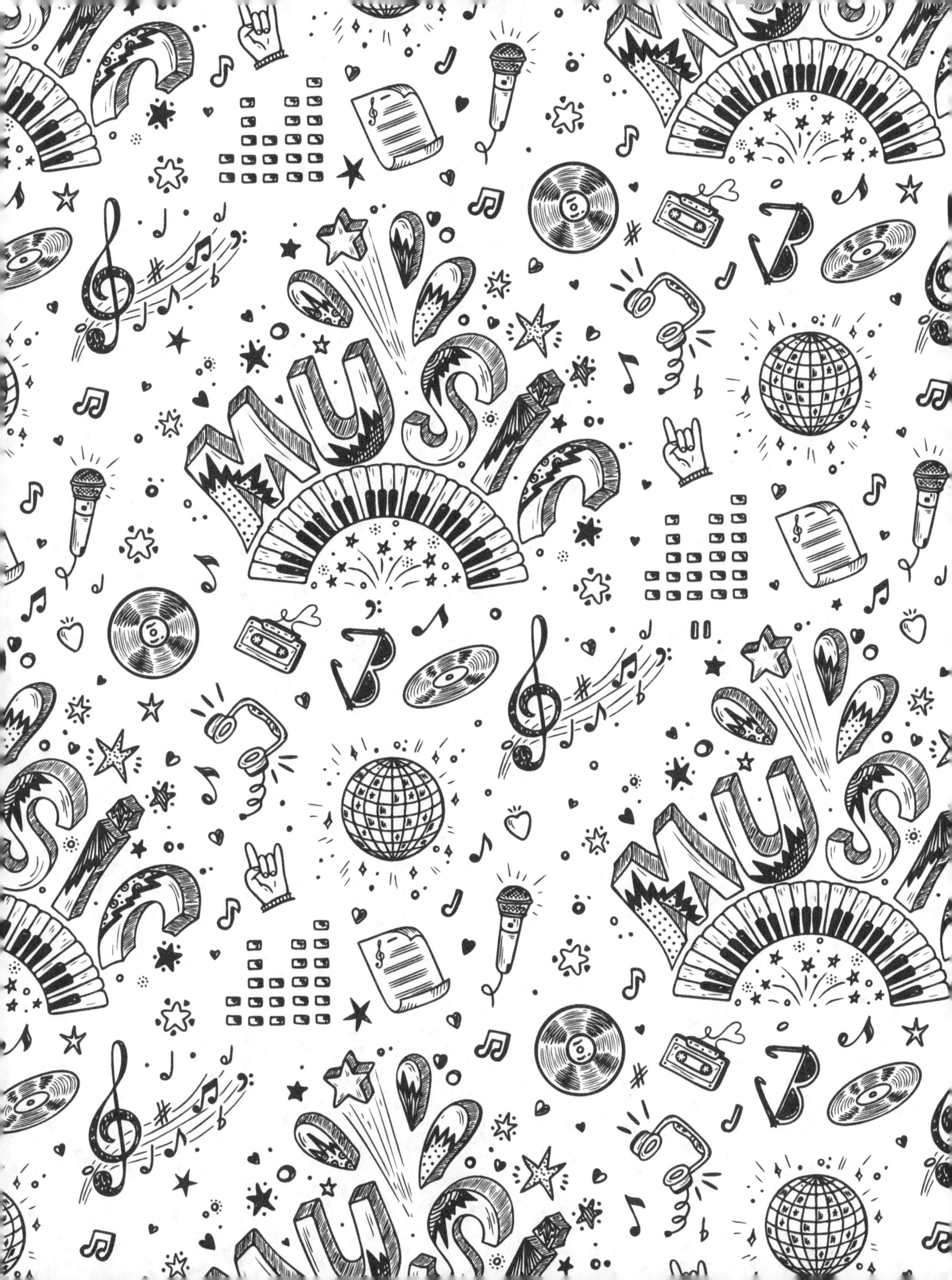

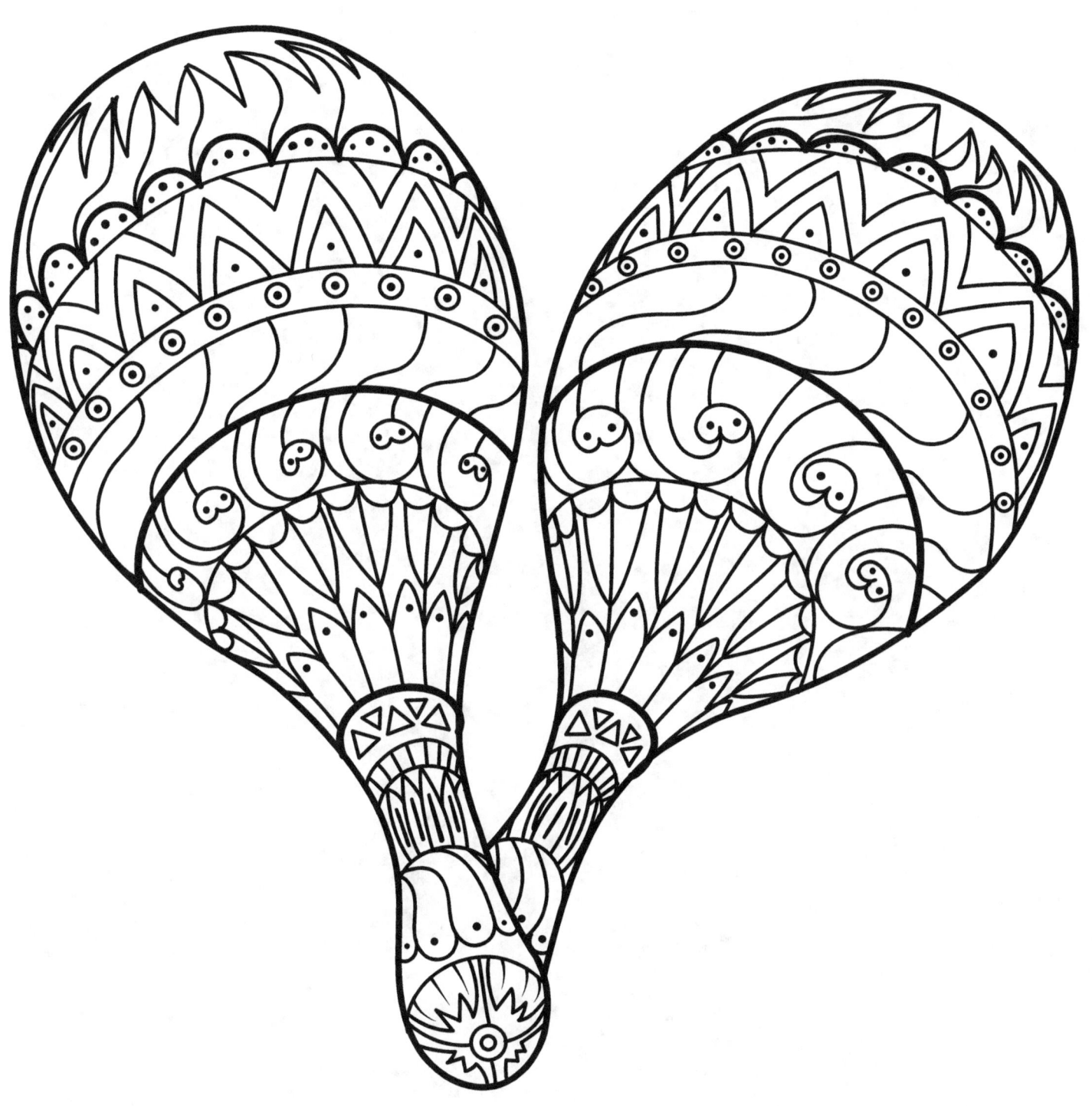

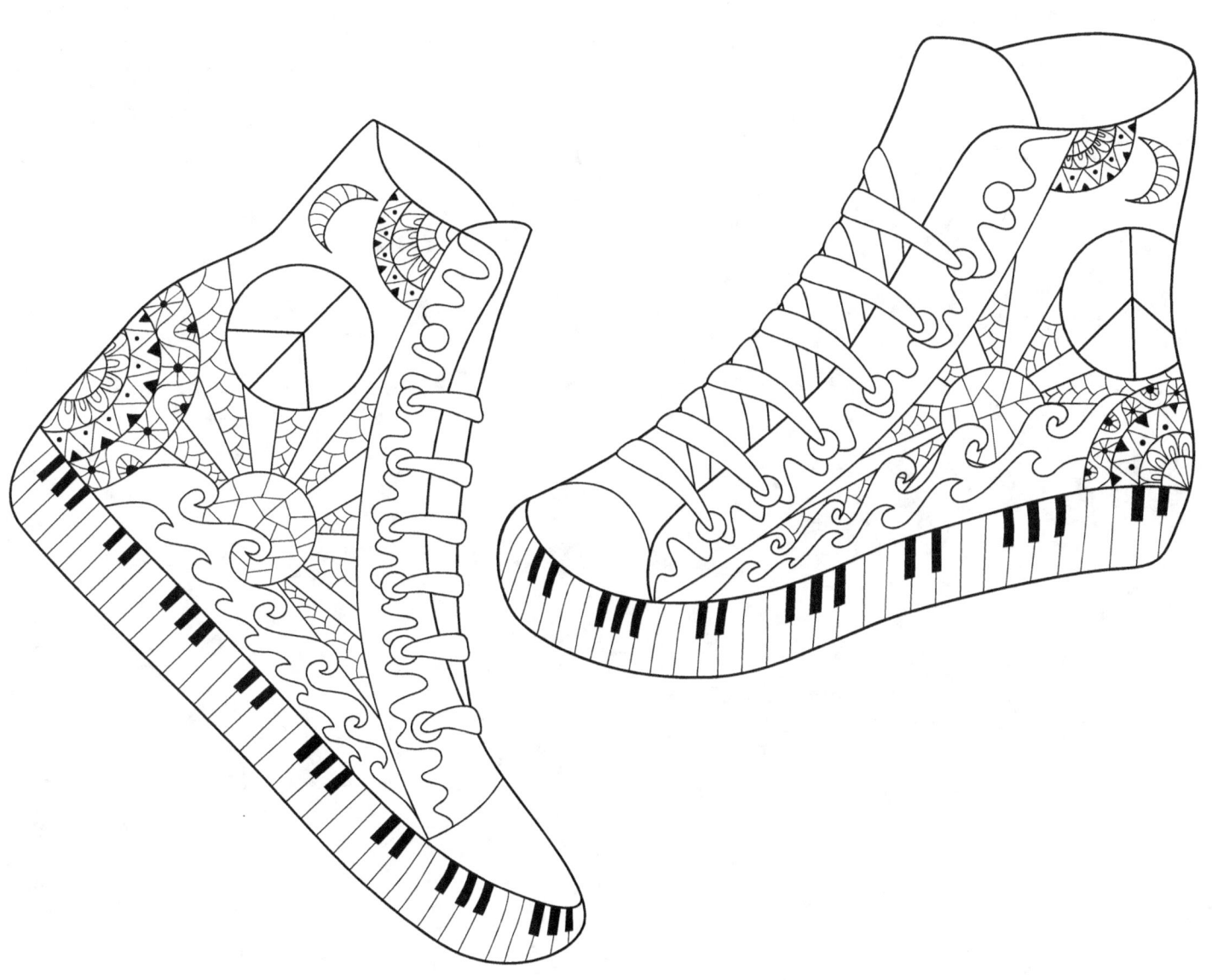

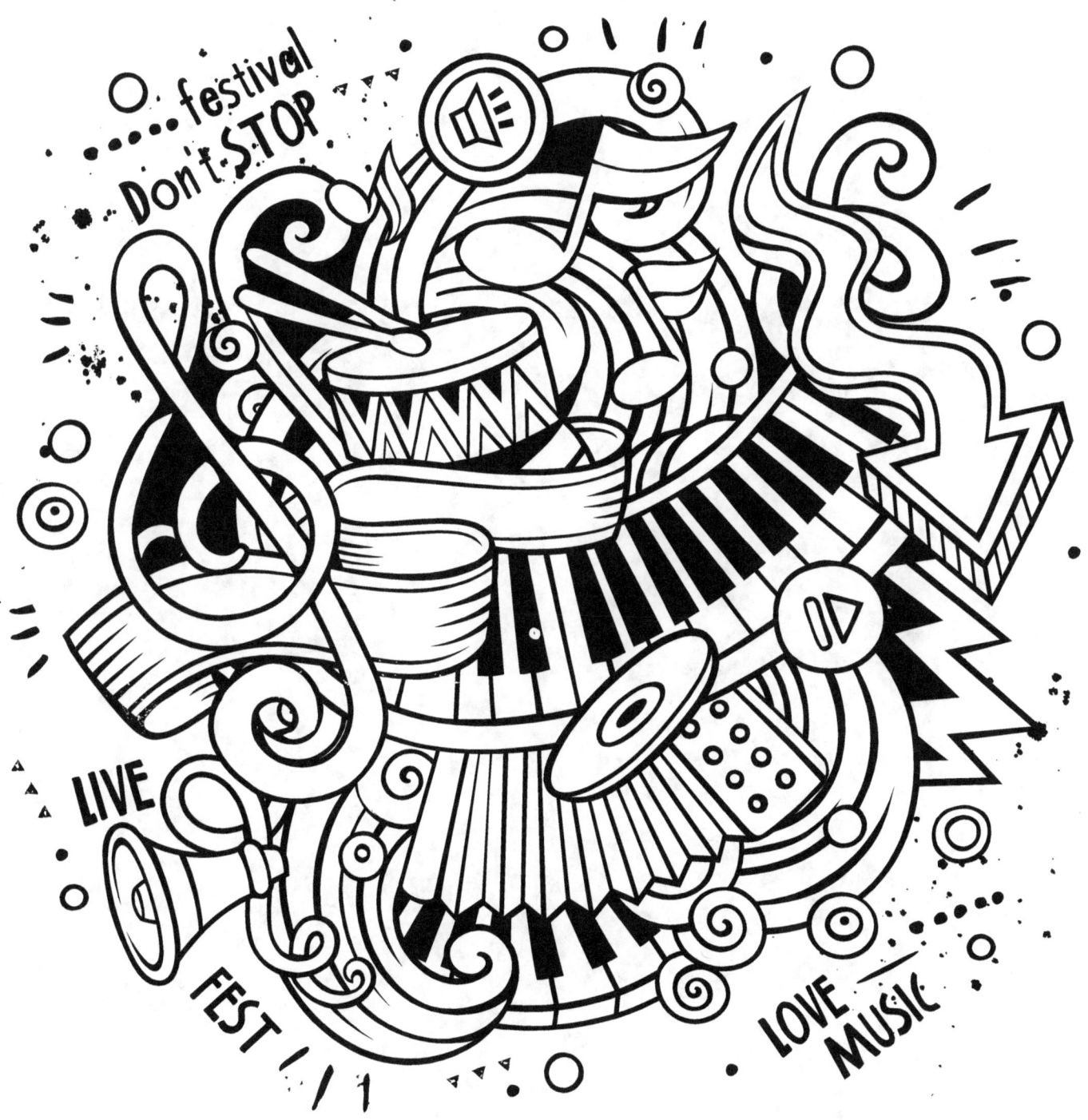

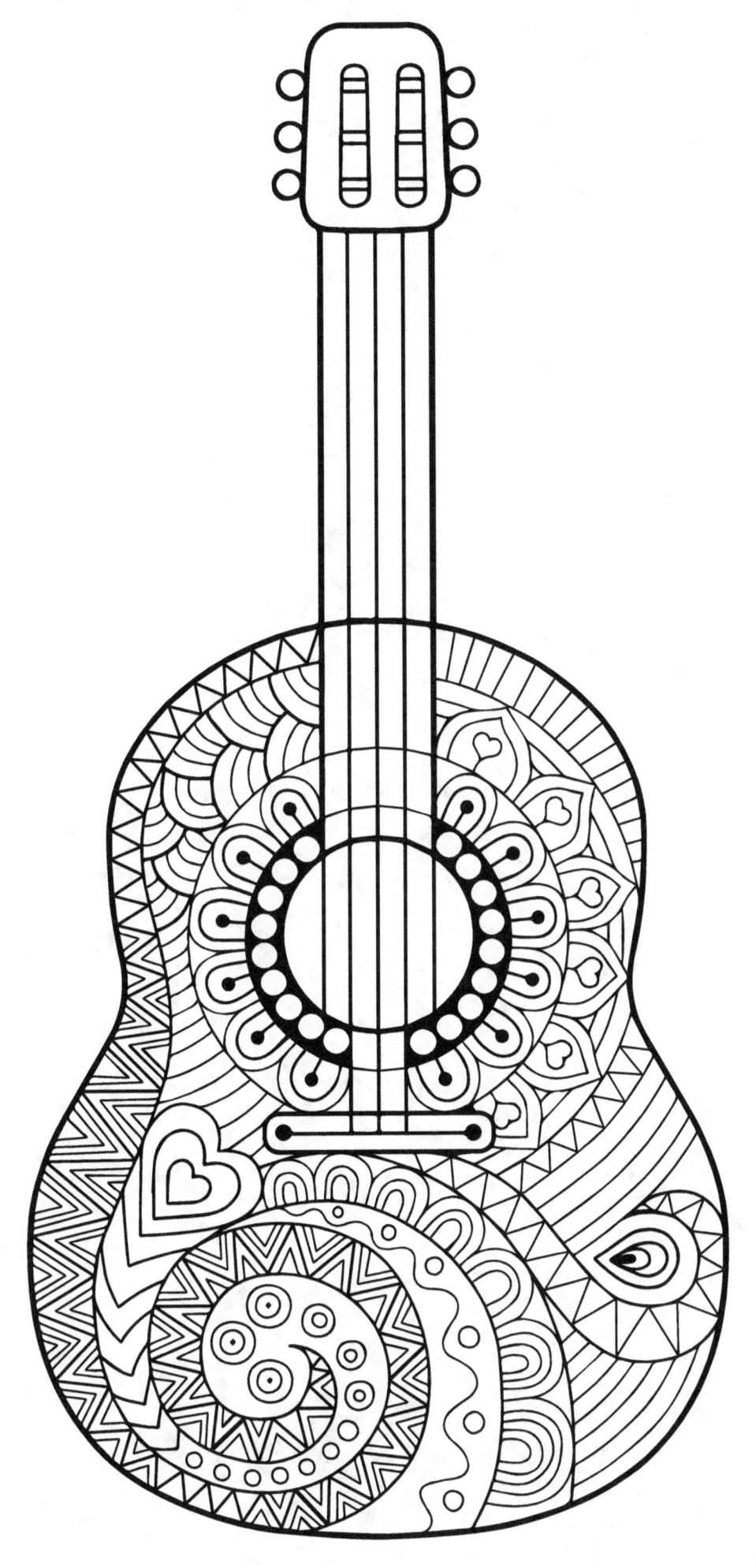

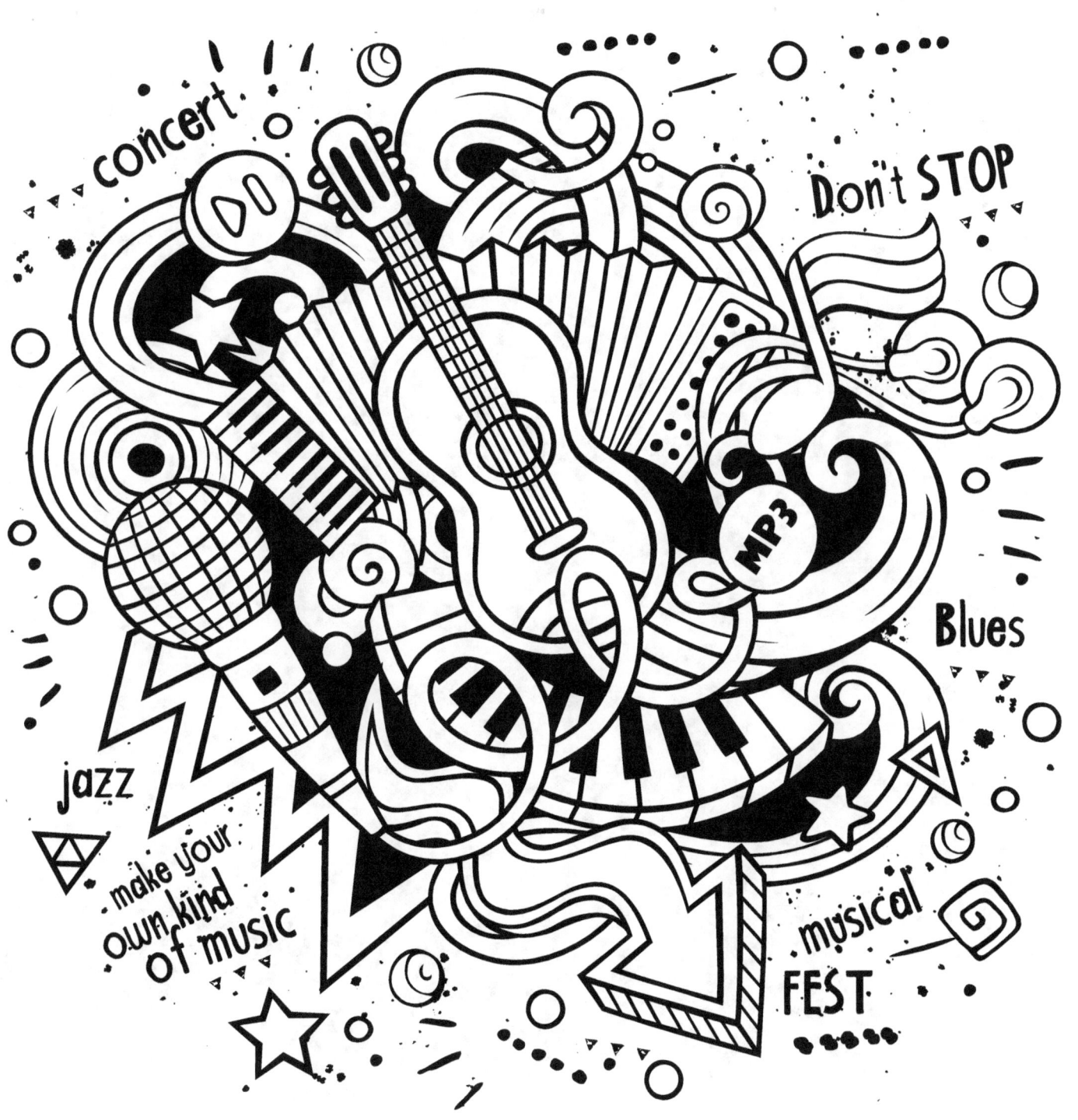

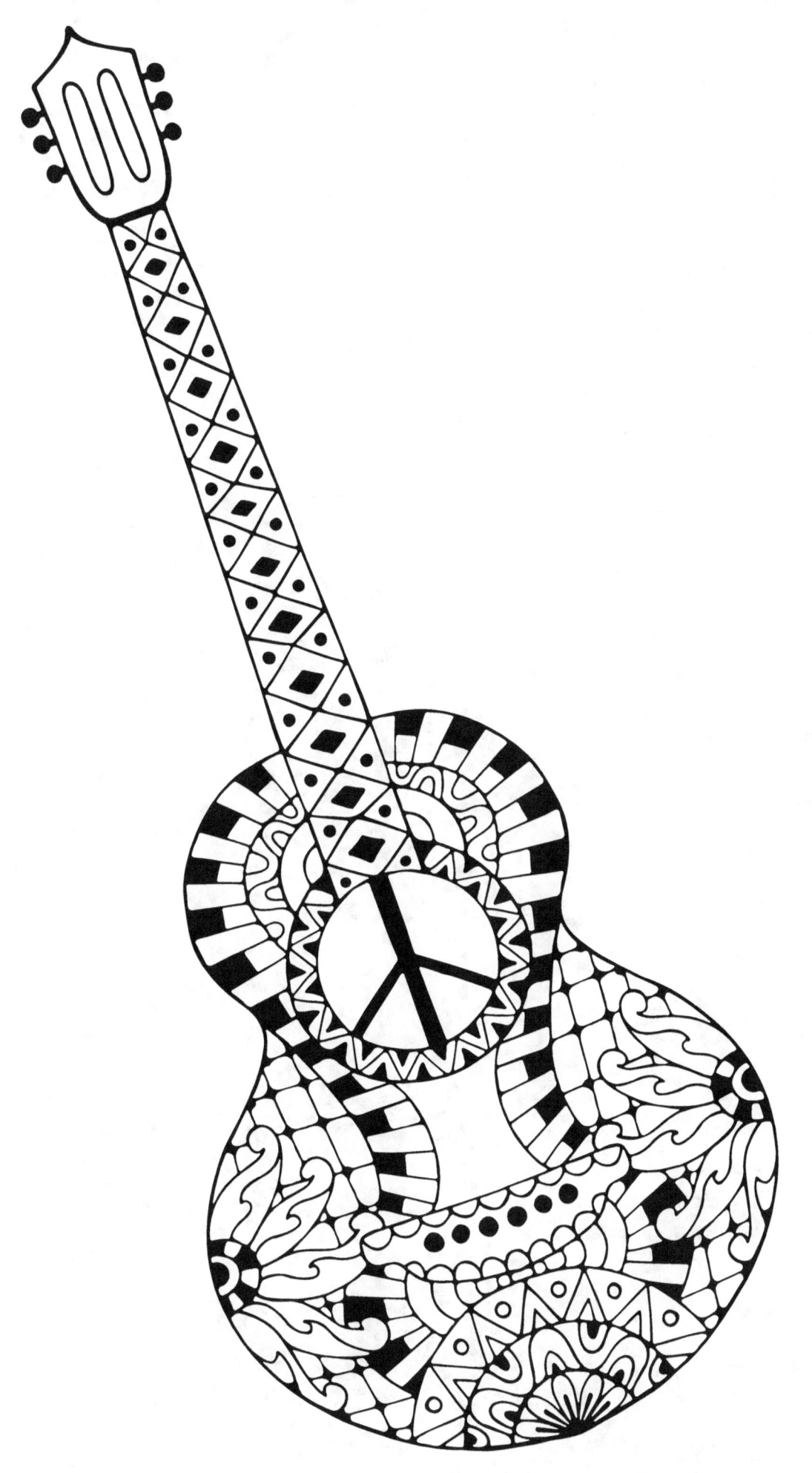

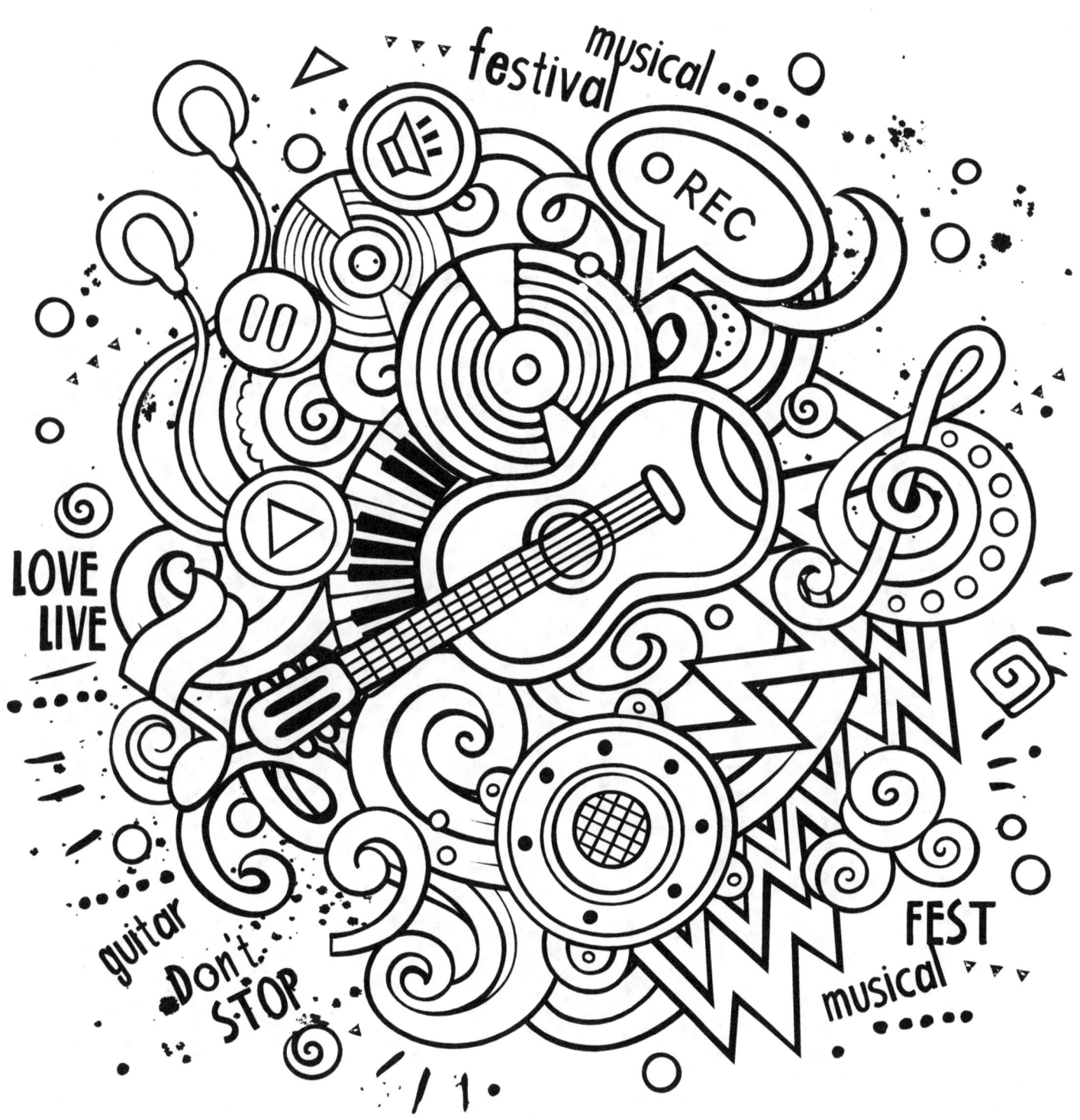

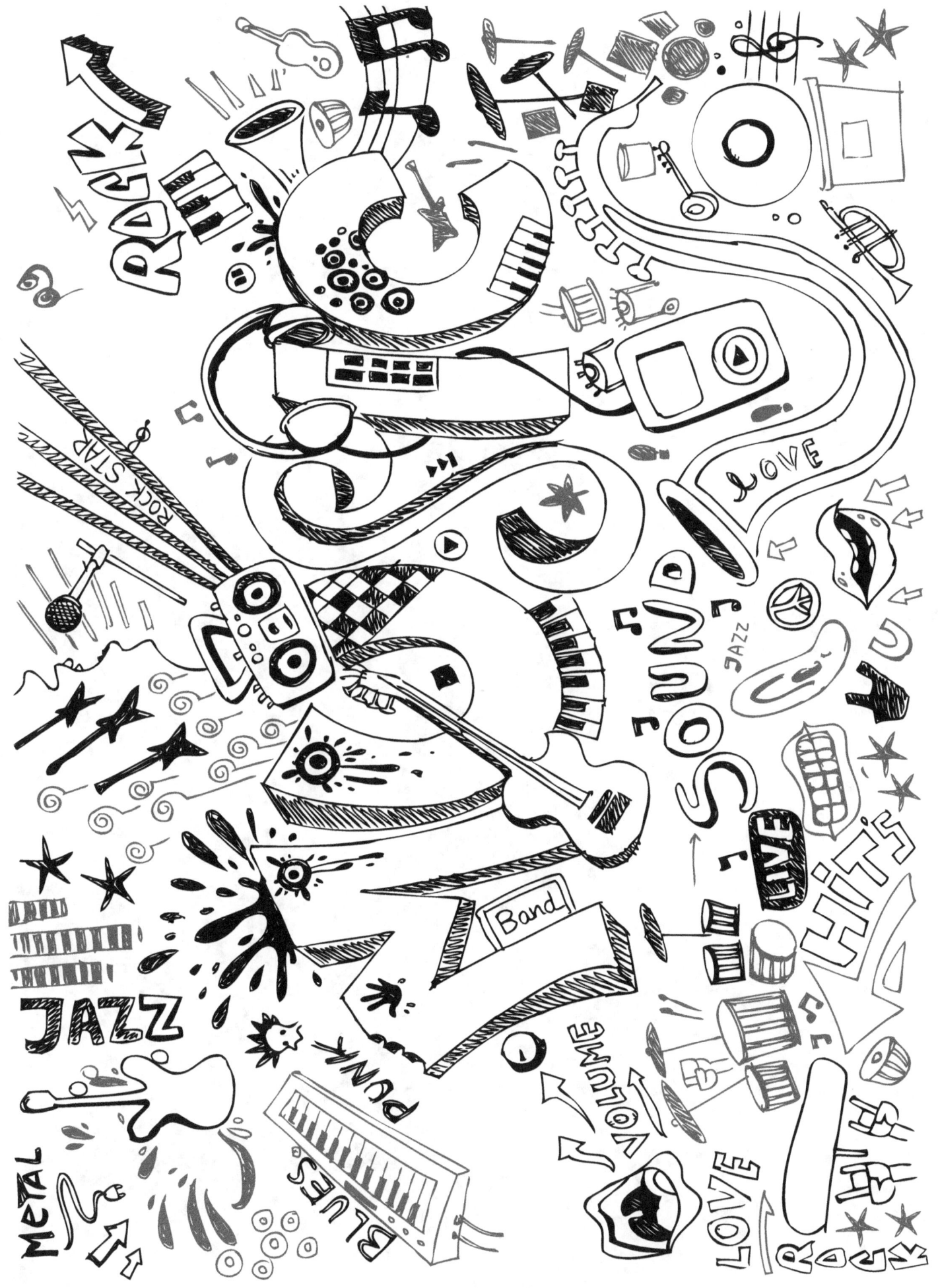

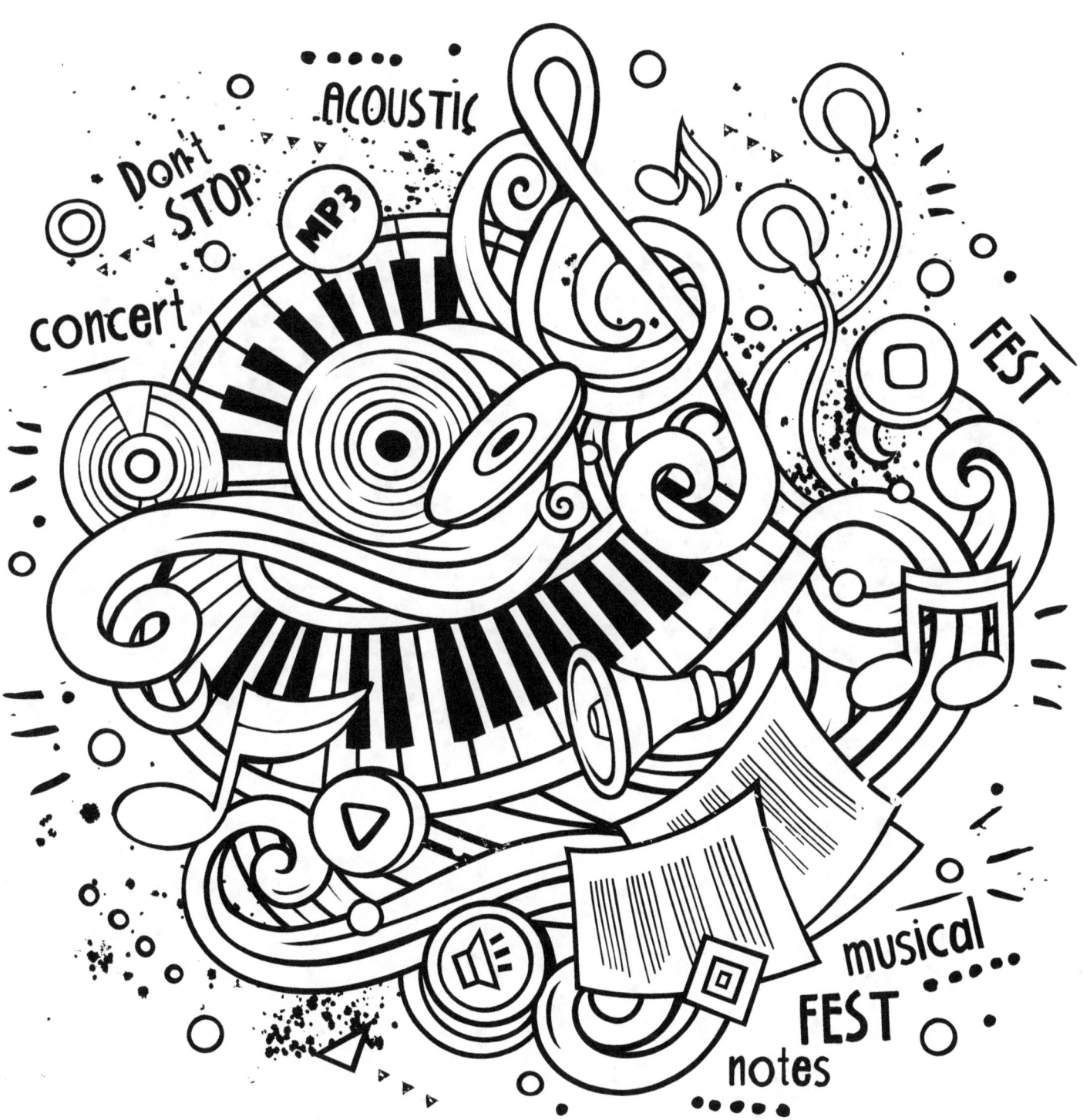

Popular Coloring Books

Coloring Books for Adults:

- Zombie Coloring Book: Black Background
- Butterfly Coloring Book For Adults: Black Background
- Tattoo Coloring Book: Black Background
- Coloring Books for Adults Relaxation: Native American Inspired Designs
- Fishing Coloring Book for Adults: Black Background

Coloring Books for Men:

- Coloring Book for Men: Anti-Stress Designs Vol 1
- Coloring Book For Men: Fishing Designs
- Coloring Book For Men: Tattoo Designs
- Coloring Books for Men: Hunting
- Coloring Book For Men: Biker Designs

Coloring Books for Seniors:

- Coloring Book For Seniors: Nature Designs Vol 1
- Coloring Book For Seniors: Anti-Stress Designs Vol 1
- Coloring Books for Seniors: Relaxing Designs
- Coloring Book For Seniors: Floral Designs Vol 1
- Coloring Book For Seniors: Ocean Designs Vol 1

Coloring Books for Teens:

- Coloring Books For Teens: Ocean Designs
- Coloring Books For Teens: Wolves & More
- Teen Inspirational Coloring Books
- Coloring Book for Teens: Anti-Stress Designs Vol 1
- Coloring Books for Teen Girls Vol 1

Coloring Books for Kids:

- Horse Coloring Book For Girls
- Coloring Books For Boys: Sharks
- Coloring Books for Boys: Animal Designs
- Unicorn Coloring Book for Girls
- Detailed Coloring Books For Kids

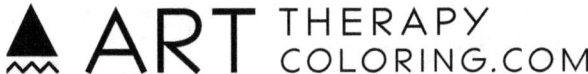

Test Your Colors

Drawing Page

Drawing Page

Drawing Page

Teen Coloring Book
Music

Published by:
Art Therapy Coloring
www.arttherapycoloring.com

Copyright © 2018 by Art Therapy Coloring
All Rights Reserved

Images Under License From Shutterstock

www.ingramcontent.com/pod-product-compliance
Lightning Source LLC
Chambersburg PA
CBHW081346180526
45171CB00006B/606